MEANING IN LIFE

BOOKS BY IRVING SINGER

Meaning in Life: The Creation of Value

The Nature of Love
1. Plato to Luther
2. Courtly and Romantic
3. The Modern World

Mozart and Beethoven: The Concept of Love in Their Operas

The Goals of Human Sexuality

Santayana's Aesthetics

Essays in Literary Criticism by George Santayana (Editor)

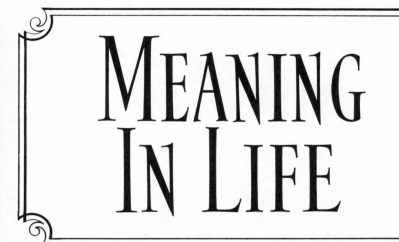

MEANING IN LIFE

The Creation of Value

IRVING SINGER

THE FREE PRESS
A Division of Macmillan, Inc. • *New York*

MAXWELL MACMILLAN CANADA
Toronto

MAXWELL MACMILLAN INTERNATIONAL
New York • *Oxford* • *Singapore* • *Sydney*

The Free Press
A Division of Macmillan, Inc.
866 Third Avenue, New York, N. Y. 10022

Maxwell Macmillan Canada, Inc.
1200 Eglinton Avenue East
Suite 200
Don Mills, Ontario M3C 3Nl

Macmillan, Inc. is part of the Maxwell Communication
Group of Companies.

Printed in the United States of America

printing number
1   2   3   4   5   6   7   8   9   10

Library of Congress Cataloging-in-Publication Data

Singer, Irving.
    Meaning in life: the creation of value / Irving Singer.
        p.   cm.
    Includes bibliographical references.
    ISBN 0-02-928905-X
    1. Life.   2. Meaning (Philosophy)   I. Title.
BD431.S578   1992   91-29401
128—dc20   CIP

To Ben

CONTENTS

Preface   xi

Introduction: Our Human Predicament   1

1
The Meaning of Life: Rephrasing Questions   17

2
The Meaning of Death   48

3
The Creation of Meaning   72

4
Lives of Meaning and Significance   101

Conclusion: The Love of Life   131

Notes   149

Index   155

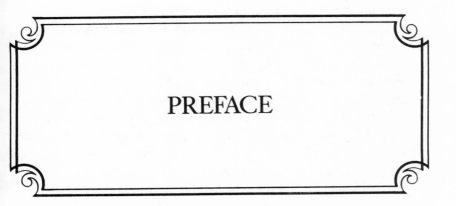

PREFACE

This book is a personal testament in the form of a philosophical exploration. Much of it can be read as an intellectual odyssey. Like many others, I turned at an early age to writings about life and meaning in the hope of finding a coherent world view consistent with my own sense of reality. I soon discovered that the sheer articulation of problems and answers in this area created major difficulties for anyone who aspires to intellectual honesty. Faced by the enormity of the issues, I felt that one needed not only pervasive humility but also a way of putting all possible theorizing into the closest rapport with one's immediate experience of the world— with vague intimations or intuitions or ideational probings that often elude precise analysis while clamoring for sympathetic understanding.

In writing about these questions, I have therefore sought to clarify, if only for myself, the cognitive twists and turns through which my thinking has evolved. Beginning with panoramic queries about "the meaning of life," I suggest that they be reconceived and redirected in order for us to learn how human beings can attain lives that are meaningful and perhaps, in a special sense that I later introduce, significant. The entire book is based on a distinction between searching for a prior meaning of life and the creating of meaning in one's life apart from any such concern. I cumulatively try to show how the latter enables us to have a life worth living.

In making this attempt, I have no arcane message to profess, no doctrine that I recognize as ultimate or authoritative for those who do not see the world as I do. Contentious as I may be and eager to refute arguments that I find challenging, I am more interested in making suggestions than in reaching definite conclusions. Studying the meaning that may be available in life, I have sought to illuminate the complexity of doubt and confusion that reflective human beings generally encounter. At the same time I also want to provide the outlines of a point of view that others can accept or reject, improve or criticize, in accordance with their own experience and predilection.

The book is not addressed to specialists in any field. It is based on a series of public lectures that I delivered in a program on medicine and the humanities at the Johns Hopkins Medical Institutions. The audience consisted of members of the general community, and most of them were not trained in philosophy or in literature—the two disciplines that overlap in my approach. My lectures were designed to convey a perspective that I have developed over a number of years, drawing on the efforts others have recently made in related fields but not pretending to represent them. In expanding and greatly revising the contents of those lectures, I have retained the initial intention and written with the same kind of audience in mind. Those who wish to do further research will find in the endnotes many references to other books and articles.

The ideas I discuss or formulate are presented mainly as tentacles that reach out and explore various problems of life and death. Having made our inquiry, we may eventually decide that some of these problems are insoluble. But that will not matter if our exploration into them is a fulfillment on its own. The outcome of philosophy is always precarious, and often unforeseeable. At least, it ought to be.

There are several people I wish to thank for the help they have provided in relation to this work. I am grateful to the Committee on Cultural and Social Affairs of the Johns Hopkins Medical Institutions, and in particular George B. Udvarhelyi and Richard A. Macksey, for having invited me to give the originating lectures. Among people who read earlier drafts of the manuscript, I am especially indebted to Herbert Engelhardt, Adam Frost, Dan Leary, and W. V. Quine. Adam Bellow, my editor at the Free Press, offered good ideas and inspired advice that I was happy to use in the final version. As always, my writing at every stage owes a great deal to the innumerable comments of my wife Josephine Singer. Finally, there are the students in courses at MIT who enriched my thinking by responding critically to it. I dedicate the finished product to my son, as a representative of their questing spirit.

I. S.

MEANING
IN LIFE

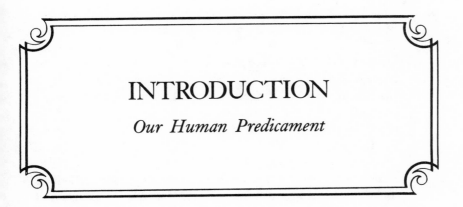

INTRODUCTION

Our Human Predicament

Throughout history educated people generally assumed that philosophy, like religion, is capable of elucidating the meaning of life. In the past, philosophers often made this attempt. But the twentieth century has been different. Questions about the meaning of life have been dismissed or neglected by many of the greatest thinkers in the last hundred years. Even if they were right to do so, we must nevertheless wonder why it is that human beings are both attracted to such matters and constantly baffled by them. I begin with a quotation from an interview that George Bernard Shaw gave in 1901. At the end of many queries about various subjects, the interviewer asks for "one word as to the meaning of the world-comedy." Shaw replies as follows:

> It is this thoughtless demand for a meaning that produces the comedy. You ask for it in one word though we are not within a million years, as yet, of seeing the world as it really is. We are

intellectually still babies: this is perhaps why a baby's facial expression so strongly suggests the professional philosopher. . . . Well, we are all still as much babies in the world of thought as we were in our second year in the world of sense. Men are not real men to us: they are heroes and villains, respectable persons and criminals. Their qualities are virtues and vices; the natural laws that govern them are gods and devils; their destinies are rewards and expiations; their reasoning a formula of cause and effect with the horse mostly behind the cart. They come to me with their heads full of these figments, which they call, if you please, "the world," and ask me what is the meaning of them, as if I or anyone else were God Omniscient and could tell them. Pretty funny this: eh? But when they ostracize, punish, murder, and make war to impose by force their grotesque religions and hideous criminal codes, then the comedy becomes a tragedy. The Army, the Navy, the Church, the Bar, the theatres, the picture-galleries, the libraries, and the trade unions are forced to bolster up their pet hallucinations. Enough. You expect me to prate about the Absolute, about Reality, about The First Cause, and to answer the universal Why. When I see these words in print the book goes into the basket. Good morning.[1]

We must all feel something similar, at least those of us who are concerned about clarity of thought. We also respond sympathetically to something Freud said, near the end of his life, in a letter to Marie Bonaparte: "The moment one inquires about the sense or value of life one is sick, since objectively neither of them has any existence. In doing so one is only admitting a surplus of unsatisfied libido."[2]

We may well agree with much of what Freud implies. A healthy person does not brood about the meaning of life. He gets up in the morning and throws himself into activities that involve his energies and provide personal gratifications. When his emotional interests are thwarted, there can be a certain amount of "unsatisfied libido" but then he will remedy the situation by taking action in some other direction. Preoccupation with the meaning of life might thus signify inefficiency in discharging libidinal excess. As Freud points out, this eventuates in "grief and depression."

In this view questions about the meaning of life have no inherent value. Presumably Freud had investigated these questions himself, or else he could not have asserted that neither the sense nor value of life has any existence "objectively." Having made his investigation, however, he was convinced that such inquiries are merely symptomatic of a pervasive sickness experienced by those who pursue them.

Later in his letter Freud admits that he may be "too pessimistic." But even if we take his comments literally, what follows from them? Since most people ask about the meaning of life at one time or other, perhaps we should conclude that the majority of human beings are sick to some extent and at crucial moments in their existence. The fact that we systematically raise unanswerable questions may indicate a form of philosophical sickness that belongs to us generically, as part of what it is to be human. In this respect Nietzsche was possibly right when he said that man is "the sick animal." To ask for the meaning of life would then be an expression of one's humanity rather than just a symptom of psychological or moral disability.

When I once mentioned Freud's idea to the philosopher W. V. Quine, he nodded in agreement with Freud. When I then quoted Nietzsche's aphorism, Quine replied: "Yes, but some of us are sicker than others." This is doubtless true. But there is no reason to think that all questioning of this sort is merely pathological. The attitude typified by the assertions of Freud and Quine ignores a dimension of cognitive exploration that many people have cherished. Human consciousness would be greatly impoverished if it eliminated its habitual concern in this area. Not only would we lessen our ability to speculate about the world, but also we would deprive ourselves of a framework within which more immediate and manageable problems can be approached. At the limits of every scientific discipline there remain troublesome issues that one cannot dismiss simply by calling them metaphysical or extra-scientific. Even if these questions are ultimately unanswerable, they elicit imaginative responses that enrich and embellish life.

To this extent an inquiry into the "sense or value" of existence does not at all indicate sickness. On the contrary, it may be the only healthy and creative way that we can express a type of curiosity distinctive to our species. Illness is generally an undesirable state of mind or body, but reflecting on the meaning of life may sometimes transmute our ontological malaise into feelings about ourselves and about the universe that integrate experience. This would be an achievement worth cultivating. To eliminate such interests is to revert to a lower order of consciousness. That path is regressive, not liberating or truly responsive to the possibilities of intellectual development.

＊

The issues that we shall be addressing are particularly urgent in our society. Though they pertain to the human condition as a whole, they also have special relevance to current attitudes. By the time the 1980s were drawing to a close, that decade was often described as a period of "instant gratification." The Western world, above all the United States, was motivated as never before by hopes of rapidly eliminating all inherent barriers between wanting something and getting it. By the beginning of the 1990s, some cultural critics argued that utopian aspirations of this sort are not only unrealistic but also conducive to facile pleasures and addictions that eventually end in demoralization. Our entire culture is often depicted as suffering from a crisis that may well undermine the values on which it is based. A large part of Western ideology, at least in the democratic traditions, has always been oriented toward giving people whatever will satisfy their desires. But how can that be justified if it means providing transient goods that foster a pervasive inability to accept and truly profit from reality?

This crisis, which now exists throughout the more advanced countries, presupposes a widespread belief that the pursuit of happiness is universal, that it can succeed in principle, and that for all men and women it is what the American Declaration of Independence calls "an inalienable right." These assumptions have guided humanistic efforts for the last two hundred years, and they reflect enlightened attitudes that are worthy of respect. It would be barbaric to suggest that people ought not to seek happiness. Nevertheless, we should consider the possibility that our current difficulties often result from a sense of meaninglessness to which favored human beings are commonly prone, and more so than those who must struggle for mere survival. If this is true, pursuing and attaining happiness might appear to be paradoxically self-defeating. The happier we are, the harder it becomes to find the meaning in our lives that is essential for remaining truly happy.

Seen from this perspective, our contemporary concern about meaning is peculiar to the modern world. It arises from our relative wealth and freedom in a context of malaise, even despair, about man's ability to achieve lasting and genuine happiness. The experience of Leo Tolstoy, who died in his eighties in 1910, can illuminate our predicament. He anticipated many of our current problems and developed solutions that are often taken for granted nowadays. His belief in passive resistance had a direct effect on Gandhi as well as Martin Luther King. But more relevant here is the emotional turmoil that uprooted his life at the age of fifty. It convinced him that his existence had no meaning and that he should terminate it as quickly as possible.

In his memoir *Confession*, Tolstoy describes the circumstances that preceded his breakdown. In some respects, they resemble the condition of many affluent baby boomers in present-day America who feel a sense of emptiness even though they may have satisfied their own personal ambitions and lived up to the demands of their society. Having succeeded in a profession, and possibly in the raising of a family, they begin to wonder obsessively about the choices they have made. They are perturbed by the possibility that their lives may really be "meaningless." This preoccupation often becomes a painful midlife crisis.

For some fifteen years Tolstoy had enjoyed the warmth and security of family happiness. He had numerous children and a wife who was devoted to him and to his work. He was recognized as the greatest living Russian author. He was wealthy, a member of the nobility, a man whose every word was listened to with great attention throughout the world. But then, as he tells us, he started experiencing "moments of bewilderment, when my life would come to a halt, as if I did not know how to live or what to do."[3] These moments turned into a continuous fixation. For weeks, months, even years he could not free himself of doubts and anxieties that weakened his composure. When he thought of what he had achieved, what he was doing, what his plans for the future involved, he could not help asking himself: What is it for? Where does it lead? What does it matter to me? He could find no answer to such questions and he began to feel that he could not live any longer. "I could breathe, eat, drink, and sleep; indeed, I could not help but breathe, eat, drink, and sleep. But there was no life in me because I had no desires whose satisfaction I would have found reasonable."[4]

Tolstoy also tells us that his prodigious powers of physical and mental exertion remained unabated. He labored in the fields with his peasants as he had before, and he continued to pursue his intellectual labors for eight and ten hours a day without ill effects. But he was wracked by what he calls a "fear of life." He felt that life had no meaning whatsoever. It led to a complete annihilation which he dreaded yet felt he should hasten through suicide. He says he hid a rope for fear that he would hang himself in his room, and he stopped going out to shoot lest he suddenly turn the gun on himself. "I myself did not know what I wanted. I was afraid of life, I struggled to get rid of it, and yet I hoped for something from it."[5]

As a way of alleviating this mental agony, Tolstoy turned to philosophy and science for answers to the questions that tormented him. He soon concluded that science systematically avoids matters related to the meaning of life and that all persuasive arguments in philosophy served to prove that life can have no meaning. Studying the greatest thinkers of the past—he mentions Socrates, Schopenhauer, Solomon (Ecclesiastes), and Buddha—he felt that they merely confirmed his own negative conclusions. They too seemed convinced that life is pointless, that it has no goal beyond itself, that despite the many casual delights that induce us to prolong our existence, we should welcome death as a release from the sheer futility of everything.

Having found nothing in science or philosophy to cure his distress, Tolstoy next asked himself how other people managed, particularly those who were educated like himself and capable of living in the manner to which he was accustomed. He observed that such people generally took one of four ways out of their difficulty. The first defense was simple ignorance about life's lack of meaning. Persons who had not yet reached his own level of sophistication might still have access to this. They appeared to enjoy rudimentary pleasures, but he was sure that he could not learn much from them. The second way out he calls "epicureanism." Assuming that life has no meaning, most cultivated people clung to their privileges and luxuries in order to preserve the gratuitous advantages that had befallen them. Though they knew it was only through good luck that they could savor whatever enjoyments were available, they merely sought further distractions in an attempt to ignore the horrifying truth. Tolstoy tells us that such deceptiveness issued from "moral dullness" and a lack of imagination which was foreign to his nature: "I could not imitate these people, since I did not lack imagination and could not pretend that I did."[6]

The third way of dealing with life's problems that Tolstoy lists is suicide. He calls this the path of "strength and energy," and he says that once a person realizes life is not worth living—as he himself believed at this point—killing oneself is "the most worthy means of escape."[7] The fourth posture was the one that he himself exemplified. He characterizes it as "weakness." Though he was sure that death was preferable to any further life, he somehow endured, hoping without reason that a meaning would become manifest in one fashion or another. Tolstoy remarks that this attitude "was disgusting and painful to me, but I remained in it all the same."[8]

It is remarkable that, in sketching these four modes of response, Tolstoy says nothing about people in his immediate society who were both imaginative and capable of truly enjoying their condition as human beings. He seems to assume that every sensitive person must have been miserable and quivering on the brink of suicide just as he was. Speaking sociologically, we may well insist that this is quite improbable.

In his memoir, Tolstoy says that he now understands why he did not commit suicide. He tells us that he clung to life not just out of weakness, but because he somehow intuited the "invalidity" of his thinking. Instead of depending entirely on his rational faculty, as he had been doing, he began to see that reason is only a partial aspect of one's being. At a deeper level there was a force he calls his "consciousness of life."[9] Intellectuals who relied on a filigree of reason to sustain themselves were not representative of mankind.

Most people, he now believed, avoid despair and find some kind of meaning in existence by retaining frequent contact with their consciousness of life. It was as if ordinary folk, the peasants above all, had an "irrational knowledge" that he and his equals had throttled in themselves. The peasants had a harder life; they suffered from physical deprivation and were denied many of the pleasures that came so easily to more fortunate individuals; yet they had access to a vital sustenance that made it impossible for them to think that life has no meaning. Without much schooling and without systematic thought, they had learned how to live in a manner that eluded him. They acted out of faith rather than reason, and he concluded that only faith comparable to theirs could make life meaningful.

From this, Tolstoy inferred that for him—and in general for anyone who had developed as he had—the only solution consisted in harmonizing his rational nature with some kind of faith that would enable him to go on living. He could not eradicate the habits of reasoning that had accumulated throughout the years and indeed defined his own particular talent. He could not pretend that he was just another peasant who blindly accepts whatever a secular or ecclesiastic authority promulgates. But unless he found a faith that resembled the irrational knowledge so many peasants had, he was sure that he would not attain the strength of life he desperately sought.

Tolstoy says that he came to love poor and simple folk, and that he gradually succeeded in learning how to emulate their attitude toward life. He states that this helped him toward religious feelings he thought he had long outgrown. The peasants' faith in God was fundamentally the same Christian faith that he had imbibed from early childhood. He had turned away from it because his reason rejected its dogmatic superstitions. He had also noticed that priests and others in the church often used religion as an excuse for self-indulgence. Living as the peasants did, he now found that orthodox views no longer seemed repellent. For a while his religious conversion led him to rejoin the Russian Orthodox church, and even to accept dogmas that had previously been most offensive to his reason.

At a later stage Tolstoy once again rebelled against orthodox theology, while still trying to remain a Christian. He reverted to the teachings of the gospels as the unquenchable source for the faith he admired in the peasants. Though he was excommunicated by the church, he thought he had finally discovered the meaning of life. By renouncing the illogical assertions of the dominant religion, he could satisfy his reason; by having faith in a supreme deity who both enacts and ordains a love of mankind, he felt united with the consciousness of life that propelled him forward from moment to moment.

Tolstoy's struggles have been interpreted in different ways. Most biographers see him, in this period of his life, as a Christian reformer who sought to cleanse Christianity of extraneous elements. Some place him in the long line of mystics who trusted their religious experience more than they trusted the institutional proclamations of the church. Nowadays adherents to various sects can find in his pacifist and humanitarian beliefs much that they consider definitive of their religion. On the other hand, Tolstoy was so troubled a human being throughout his life that clinical analyses of his conversion may also be justified.

At least one psychiatrist has argued that Tolstoy was undergoing the kind of severe depression or melancholia that frequently occurs in midlife. Men who have had great successes, who have been as virile and sexually active as Tolstoy was, often feel that life loses all its meaning once their libidinal potency declines.

Like him, they sometimes have a devastating fear of death while also thinking that suicide may be the only remedy for their condition. Even if they are able to work out a viable adjustment, as Tolstoy seems to have done, preoccupation with ultimate philosophical questions is in their case largely displacement behavior masking the emotional disturbance that besets them at this stage in life.[10]

As I shall later argue, this interpretation seems too extreme, and overly reductive. It can hardly discredit Tolstoy's belief that his conversion was authentic as well as being crucial for his continued existence. Who is to say that even the most commendable of religious attitudes may not occur in persons who are psychologically diseased? For our purposes, Tolstoy's example is interesting as an early version of what many people in our society experience despite their previous accomplishments, perhaps even because of them. Whether or not Tolstoy's solution is acceptable to us (it is not acceptable to me), his search for meaning can serve as an introduction to the modern world. As he did, we may have lingering doubts about many optimistic tenets that our parents or grandparents found convincing. We too may feel that possibly pessimists are right, or nearer to the truth, when they maintain that life is really just a tragedy.

❋

The seventeenth-century philosopher Thomas Hobbes said that in its "natural condition" the life of man is "solitary, poor, nasty, brutish, and short."[11] Hobbes thought that civilization could remedy many of the limitations in our being, and he himself lived cheerfully into his nineties. Nevertheless, he believed that we best understand human existence when we place it within a context of general adversity. In a similar vein, Francis Bacon's essay "On Adversity" points out the advantages of seeing life in its somber rather than its brighter aspects. As with "needleworks and embroideries," Bacon says, "it is more pleasing to have a lively work upon a sad and solemn ground, than to have a dark and melancholy work upon a lightsome ground."

To approach life as a tragedy in which we all participate may be a wholesome beginning even though it is only a partial perspective. It is often useful to assume a worst-case scenario. The result may not be as "pleasing" as Bacon suggests, but it can possibly have a fortifying effect that helps us to endure in a satisfactory manner. The lives of most men and women have always been difficult—liable to moral, mental, and physical suffering, and either too long (for those who find no point in it) or too short (for those who do). Large numbers of people in the twentieth century have rejected the simplicity and assurance of almost every optimistic dogma. In earlier ages they might have hoped that all human losses would somehow be regained—if not in the physical world, then in another realm that various doctrines described as the ontological basis of our own reality; if not as a good to be experienced in the present, then as a utopian prospect for the future on earth or in heaven or in some mythological combination of the two.

This kind of faith is scarcely intelligible to millions in the world today. For many of us it is not a viable option. We believe, as a matter of scientific fact, that life on this planet is an unusual and possibly unique phenomenon occurring within a cosmic setting that may otherwise be an enormous wasteland. We also believe that the character as well as the continuance of life is ultimately governed by material forces beyond the control of any conscious being. The universe would appear to be nothing but a field of energy. Eventually everything that now exists may totally dissolve, as Prospero says in Shakespeare's *Tempest*, and "leave not a rack behind."

More than any of its predecessors, our generation may therefore feel that life is not only a tragedy but also one that we perform before an empty house. Within the overall experience there can be incidental types of gratification, as there are for actors in a play. Some people find contentment in life by limiting their attention to consummations that satisfy their sensory and emotional needs without greatly taxing their intellect. If they are lucky and have been spared financial pressures while remaining in good health, they may even taste what the Italians call *il dolce far niente* (the sweetness of doing nothing). For many people this version of earthly paradise is all they want, though it is usually reserved for life after retirement.

Others seek, and sometimes find, a period of happiness that differs from mere contentment. In its ability to satisfy a wider range of interests, social as well as personal and active as well as passive, happiness bespeaks a harmony between the separate individual and his or her environment. It includes intervals of pleasure, but is more characteristically a general sense of well-being and efficiency in getting what we want. At moments of great achievement or success, we may also experience that burst of positive feeling for which we use words like "joy" or "ecstasy."

These gratifications are not trivial aspects of the human condition, as pessimists in philosophy have often claimed. Though we shall mainly be concerned with questions about meaning, we need not doubt the importance of contentment, happiness, and joy. But even in their own dimension, these brighter possibilities that everyone desires may amount to something less than one might have expected. Pleasures quickly fade and are hard to recapture; contentment often degenerates into boredom and a bovine weariness with life; permanent happiness is evasive not only because we are easily deluded in our hunger for anything that might make us happy, but also because our quest depends on external circumstances that can cease to cooperate at any moment. Aristotle rightly said: call no man happy while he is still alive.

As for joy, that summit of our affective being idealized by nineteenth-century romanticism as a virtual infusion of divinity, even those who must know the experience best find it to be infrequent and unpredictable. We may think that creative men and women have the greatest access to beauty and to joy. And yet, regardless of what has been achieved, an artist must always face the agonies of each particular art form. These present themselves anew in every work, and they inevitably curtail any momentary joyfulness. Joy may register the completion of what we have done in the past, but it does not guarantee that we shall be able to continue. The geniuses who have so clearly earned the reward of joy or ecstasy are precisely the ones who suffer most acutely from the constant struggles that creativity involves. Life is not a path of determinate length and direction such that creative individuals who have traveled furthest can feel that they are closer to some absolute and all-resolving goal. The past cannot be relived, and the future is never fully knowable until it becomes the present. The more that human beings accomplish, the more they generally realize how little they have done.

Still we may feel that the great achievers are people who have the most meaningful and significant existence. Surely they are best equipped to show us what life can yield. Even if life is tragic, do they not reveal how it can be turned into a work of art—not a comedy, perhaps, or even a melodrama that has a happy ending, but a tragedy that plumbs the depths? Tragedies impose mythic and aesthetic coordinates upon some particular reality chosen for imaginative re-creation. Is it too much to hope that human beings can deal with all of life that way?

※

Few of our major philosophers in the twentieth century have had much to say about these questions. Particularly in the traditions that have dominated philosophy in the English-speaking countries, problems concerning the meaning of life were largely ignored until recent years. In one place, however, Ludwig Wittgenstein makes some brief remarks that are worth considering. After asserting that "the meaning of life, i.e. the meaning of the world, we can call God," he offers the following reflections:

> Dostoievsky is right when he says that the man who is happy is fulfilling the purpose of existence.
>
> Or again we could say that the man is fulfilling the purpose of existence who no longer needs to have any purpose except to live. That is to say, who is content.
>
> The solution of the problem of life is to be seen in the disappearance of this problem. . . .

> But is it possible for one so to live that life stops being problematic? That one is *living* in eternity and not in time?
>
> Isn't this the reason why men to whom the meaning of life had become clear after long doubting could not say what this meaning consisted in?[12]

Wittgenstein intimates that those who know the meaning of life may reveal it in how they live, although they find themselves unable to analyze its components. This is surely true, since experience—particularly affirmative and satisfying experience—does not always lend itself to detailed examination. To say, however, that "the solution" to the problem of life involves its disappearance leaves open the possibility of a definite resolution that might someday enable philosophers to discard this problem entirely. Wittgenstein does wonder whether one could ever live in such a way that life would stop being problematic, but he seems to think that this can occur for those who are happy or content or no longer depend on "any purpose except to live."

But all of this requires much more discussion than Wittgenstein provides. Not only do we need greater clarification about the meaning of concepts such as "purpose" or "living in eternity," but we must also decide what kind of "problem" the problem of life can possibly be. Philosophical problems are not always solvable. How do we determine whether or not problems about the meaning of life can be resolved? Even if they cease to trouble us, can we know that we have found a solution? Is it not possible that we have merely slipped into a manner of living that sedates our probing sensibilities?

Above all, we must ask ourselves whether we understand what the original problem was. Do we really know what we are requesting when we ask for a meaning of life and wonder whether or not it is inherently tragic? Possibly the greatest difficulty consists not in finding a solution but in elucidating the meaning of our questions. When Gertrude Stein was dying, her friend Alice B. Toklas is reported to have said, "Gertrude, Gertrude, what is the answer?" Miss Stein replied: "Alice, Alice, what is the question?"

As another illustration, consider a passage in *The Hitchhiker's Guide to the Galaxy* by Douglas Adams. The computer named Deep Thought announces that he has finally determined the meaning of life and that, by his calculation, the answer to the great question is forty-two. The humanoids who have been eagerly awaiting his findings, generation after generation for seven and a half million years, are thunderstruck. They had expected a different kind of answer to the "Ultimate Question of Life, the Universe and Everything." But Deep Thought explains that their problem arises from their confusion about the question. "So once you do know what the question is," he says, "you'll know what the answer means."[13]

It should be noted that Deep Thought has nothing else to say about the answer. He only claims that knowing the question will enable us to know what the answer means. This seems to me like the beginning of wisdom about the nature of philosophy. If we expect our inquiry to provide definitive and satisfying solutions, we are likely to be disappointed. Each of its answers, assuming they are fertile and not stillborn in themselves, will always generate new problems that must also be resolved. Though philosophy can stimulate the imagination and lead to intellectual advances, its greatest benefit consists in encouraging us to clarify our intuitions. We all know what reality is, Socrates said, because we are all equally immersed in it. But most of us have confused ideas about ourselves and about the world. Through philosophy, however, we may fabricate what I. A. Richards called "speculative instruments." These can help us to straighten out our thinking.

Plato and other philosophers were less cautious than Socrates, and perhaps philosophy can do more than merely give clues about how to make our ideas clear. Nevertheless, that is where we must start this kind of exploration. Before we can try to look for solutions, we must first determine which are the intelligible problems. Even if we say, as one troubled youth did, "To be or not to be: that is the question," we need to understand the nature of all such questioning.

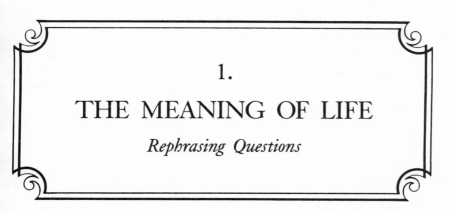

1.

THE MEANING OF LIFE

Rephrasing Questions

To a large extent, questions about the meaning of life emanate from the body of continuous investigation that constitutes the history of philosophy. And within that history, one finds an ambivalence that also pervades the mentality of ordinary people who have thought about this cluster of basic problems. We long to know the secrets of the universe and what it means, in itself, apart from human interests. At the same time, however, we seek a meaningful way to live our lives, whether or not we can find a separate meaning in the cosmos.

These two types of questions, which have usually been lumped together by philosophers as well as laymen, are really very different. Even the twentieth-century idea that life is "absurd" becomes more manageable once we recognize this difference. Having encountered difficulties in our search for a meaning of life as a whole, we may nevertheless hope to answer questions about the nature of a meaningful life. Is it something we find or something we create? How is it dependent on purposes, values, ideals? How is it related to happiness, and does it give us assurance that men and women can face up to their predicament as finite creatures? In working at these issues, we may be able to construct an outlook that reveals a life worth living even if we remain partly pessimistic about human existence.

As a prelude, it may be useful to review the speculations of three nineteenth-century philosophers who foresaw many of the problems that will follow us into the twenty-first century. Despite their dialectical differences, Hegel, Schopenhauer, and Nietzsche make a unity within themselves. On points of detail their views are often remarkably similar. Each was convinced that nothing of life, and certainly no human being, can long survive in itself. They hold out little hope for personal immortality or the escape from death that Western religions promised.

In other ways, of course, their philosophies differ greatly. Unlike the two later thinkers, Hegel is an optimist and an idealist insofar as he believes that reality is meaningful as a totality. Though individuals are annihilated once they have played their tiny role, they all contribute to the ongoing development of the cosmos. They do so by searching for value and self-awareness. Hegel identifies this quest, which he considers fundamental in the universe, as a yearning for moral or spiritual goals. This striving explains the material order of things as well as the struggles of conscious beings. Hegel believes that all reality moves toward total union with absolute spirit. Such union is also *re*union since it entails a return to primordial oneness, though each new particularity undergoes a kind of separation merely in existing as itself.

If Hegel is right, life may well be called a tragedy for everything that participates in it. It is tragic for each entity perceived as a being whose organic drives and cherished values will be defeated sooner or later. But in contributing to the search for greater spirituality, which motivates their behavior whether or not they realize it, all things have a permanent place within the cosmic performance. Their tragic existence contains an inherent creativity that reveals the progressive attainment of ever-increasing meaningfulness, goodness, and beauty.

Since Hegel assures us that these ideal determinants are objectively present in the world, we might well conclude that life is not really tragic. Taken as a whole it would all seem to be an ontological comedy, an enterprise that justifies our deepest hopes. It is nevertheless a tragedy for the participants, since they survive their brief appearance only in having a meager effect upon the ineluctable flow that quickly engulfs them. One might therefore say that Hegel sees life as a tragi-comedy: tragic for those who perform in it but infinitely rewarding for the evolving and impersonal spirituality that marches toward fulfillment throughout this process.

In its own sophisticated manner, the Hegelian comedy of life resembles the divine comedy that Dante portrays. In the *Paradiso* the blessed spirits are not entities of the sort they were on earth. In effect they have been annihilated, as Hegel would also say, for now they have no being apart from God. They radiate his luminous goodness, from which they are no longer separated. But in their unity with God, are they really persons? Are they not merely resplendent expressions of the divine presence? Hegel seems to think so. He duplicates Dante's vision except that he sees the final beatitude as residual or latent in each moment, as operative in existence at all times. For him this pervasive spirituality shows forth the meaning of life and explains the being of anything that occurs.

Schopenhauer, who was Hegel's contemporary, opposes his philosophy and condemns it as hideous wish-fulfillment. He denies that there is any benign principle in the cosmos that can mitigate or justify the suffering one observes. Schopenhauer thinks that all life must be tragic, since every event is governed by laws of nature that have nothing in them that could be considered ideal. The fundamental principle existing in the universe is dynamic, material, brutal, non-purposive, and more or less without direction. Schopenhauer calls this principle "the will" since we feel it most directly in our volitional impulses.

Rejecting Hegel's faith in underlying spiritual goals, Schopenhauer argues that existence is simply a reservoir of energy spewing out in no meaningful pattern—like explosions in an atom or a distant galaxy. Nature germinates individual manifestations of itself but then reamalgamates them without a trace, everything that exists belonging to an enormous recycling process. The totality keeps changing but without any discernible rationale. In living things, only an instinct for self-preservation is constant. At times, Schopenhauer refers to the will as "the will to live." Nothing else could count as an explanation of life.

Schopenhauer believes that animate existence is more often a form of suffering than of happiness or pleasure. Life on earth is a calamity whose only cure is death. But though he is pessimistic in this respect, he also thinks that knowledge of his philosophy will help us live agreeable and rewarding lives. Once people understand that the metaphysical will to which they are subject is unconcerned about their welfare, they can adapt to this fatality in constructive and satisfying ways. They cannot defeat the will and they must reconcile themselves to being parts of a recycling process. But also they can show their revulsion at the mindless cruelty of existence and attain essential dignity in their reaction to it.

Schopenhauer articulates a system of meaningful responses to the tragedy of life, and he outlines a moral philosophy based on feeling compassion for the suffering of everything that lives. The sense of dignity, which he posits as the source of any possible salvation, results from various attitudes or attainments that he recommends: philosophical awareness provided by his metaphysics; scientific and technological knowledge that enables us to re-direct the will despite our subjugation to it; contemplation of the quasi-Platonic forms through which, he thinks, being always shows itself; creativity and aesthetic delight that employs such contemplation in the making and enjoying of works of art; and in general, renunciation of bodily interests that merely perpetuate the will's imperious appetite.

In offering liberation of this sort, Schopenhauer's philosophy is neither gloomy nor wholly defeatist. He himself seems to have had a comfortable existence, writing as he wished, playing his flute for pleasure, and taking walks with his little dog. One can live a good or at least bearable life, he thought, but only after one has stared the horrors of reality in the face and withdrawn allegiance from the metaphysical force that produces them. Though we cannot defeat the will, we can and should say no to it. This was what Ivan Karamazov in Dostoyevsky's novel would later call giving back the ticket to the universe. Generations of thinkers who were influenced by Schopenhauer—for instance, Freud—inherited a comparable attitude of nay-saying. But it was this part of Schopenhauer's doctrine that Friedrich Nietzsche found most unacceptable as his own ideas matured.

Nietzsche agrees that the will is devoid of meaning, that it is vicious and the cause of more suffering than happiness, that there are no gods to whom we can appeal, and that the only paths of salvation are those that lead to philosophy, science, art, and the kind of morality that emerges from such pursuits. What Nietzsche could not stomach was the element of negativity in Schopenhauer's philosophy. He himself had, both mentally and physically, a more delicate constitution than Schopenhauer, and he felt that saying no to the universe would prevent one from being able to live productively.

As an alternative to nay-saying, Nietzsche recommends *amor fati* (love of destiny, or things as they really are). This attitude entails a heroic and healthy-minded acceptance of reality *even though* it is horrible and wholly destructive to everything that participates in it. For Nietzsche this love of the hateful cosmos is the highest attainment humanity can reach: "My formula for greatness in a human being is *amor fati:* that one wants nothing to be different, not forward, not backward, not in all eternity. Not merely bear what is necessary, still less conceal it—all idealism is mendaciousness in the face of what is necessary—but *love* it."[1]

Nietzsche synthesizes the philosophies of Hegel and Schopenhauer. For Hegel, existence—harsh and horrid as it often is—could only be the means by which spirit joyfully progressed. Though life was a tragedy for everything that lives, it would eventually provide a happy resolution for the totality of being. Nietzsche is convinced that this totality must be meaningless, devoid of spirit, as Schopenhauer had said. And yet he thinks participants in life might create—through amor fati—a heroic comedy by courageously accepting it all despite the fact that everything is ultimately tragic and even vile. In this way, Nietzsche feels, one might see life realistically without undermining the pursuit of noble ideals that Hegel considered paramount.

There is much in Nietzsche's philosophy that speaks to people of the twentieth century. But his ideas about amor fati and the meaning of life are unconvincing to me. If Schopenhauer was accurate in depicting the horror of all existence, as Nietzsche believed, why should one *accept* reality rather than reject it as much as possible? Why should we identify with the aggressor, so to speak, instead of hating our subjection to the will? Would it not be more honest to cry out in terror—as in the famous painting of *The Shriek* by Edvard Munch—or at least to recognize coolly that there must always remain a basic discontinuity between our values and the world in which they make their freakish and unrepresentative appearance?

Nietzsche may have thought that love is so essential that no one, not even a liberated pessimist like Schopenhauer, could enjoy a single moment of existence unless he contrived to love reality despite its utter worthlessness. He may also have felt that only one who loves the world while knowing how bad it is can find the fortitude needed to improve it through moral conduct. But if the Nietzschean philosopher-saint loves everything that exists, how can he reject the bad elements? The worst parts of existence also belong to reality, and he has determined to love and therefore to accept it all completely. Nietzsche's synthesis of Schopenhauer and Hegel is, at best, very problematic.[2]

Hegel's optimism may seem ridiculous to us in view of its unswerving certitude about the goodness of the universe, but it alerts us to the importance of ideals and to the human capacity for self-fulfillment in the act of pursuing them. Hegel's greatest strength consists in his recognition that human beings can and do enjoy life by striving for spiritual goals. Consummation of this sort presupposes an attunement to nature and the world in which we live. Hegel understood that we could not have the ends, the interests, and the values that define our being unless we believed that reality sustains us in some way. Schopenhauer's philosophy is weak precisely at this point, though it is clear-sighted about the material context in which human idealization occurs. Combining the insights of Hegel and Schopenhauer, we need not recommend a love of all the terrible things that happen in reality—as Nietzsche's notion of amor fati requires—but we may be able to develop a view of the world that is realistic and yet sensitive to the possibility of meaning. Nietzsche is to be revered for having shown us, with greater power than anyone else, how ghastly human experience will be in the coming years unless our philosophers succeed in working out the details of a viable synthesis.

✼

But what exactly is involved in the problems we are exploring? What is one saying when one asks for the meaning of life? People who raise this question usually want to know about more than life alone. They want to know where existence "comes from." They want to know the why of it: why we are "here," and why anything—or rather everything—should be as it is.[3] To the scrupulous philosopher as well as the plain-speaking skeptic on the street, such use of language must occasion puzzlement. What can "meaning" signify in this context? Out of all the many types of linguistic usage that cluster about this term, two senses of the word "meaning" seem to me especially relevant. One of them is cognitive; the other is valuational.

When we use "meaning" in its cognitive sense, we are looking for some kind of explanation, some clarification about an occurrence or event. We hope to find out why something has the properties it has. We want to gain insight into an existing or possible state of affairs. We wish to learn about its consequences, its implications for further observation. This usage applies to the denoting of an actuality as well as to the connotative function of a word. When we say "What does it mean if water fails to boil at 212 degrees Fahrenheit?" we seek a cognitive type of meaning. The same is true when we ask for the meaning of the term "Fahren-heit."

On the other hand, we often use the word "meaning" in relation to personal feelings and emotional significance. It then reveals and sometimes declares our highest values. It manifests ideals that we cherish and pursue, that guide our behavior and provide the norms by which we live. "Friendship means a great deal to that man; when his friends have need of him, money means nothing at all." This way of using words like "means" or "meaning" is easily combined with the first kind of usage. In saying that a mother's attitude toward her child reveals the meaning of love, we are suggesting that her response exemplifies a value system that may well be studied for its cognitive import.

People who search for "the meaning of life" are trying to articulate analogous questions about the world. They want to know what would enable us to understand the diverse and frequently bizarre phenomena that constitute reality. But also they wonder whether things can be as they are because of some benign intention of a quasi-human sort that pervades the universe. Theories about a deity who has created everything are often secondary to this concern. Ideas about God's essence—whether he is infinitely wise or good or powerful—pertain to mainly technical problems in theology. To argue about the Supreme Being's attributes is to engage in an exercise that probably has minor importance for most people. William James was quite right when he claimed that the "cash value" of such deliberations resides in our primordial need to reassure ourselves about an ultimate good will in the cosmos, a basic friendliness toward us and what we value, a final haven or support for our ideals and aspirations.

James thought that the "need of an eternal moral order is one of the deepest needs of our breast."[4] Whether this is true of everyone, and whether or not the need is satisfiable, it helps explain our search for meaning in both senses of the term and regardless of specific religious belief. We know what it is to pursue ideals that express human values and elicit relevant emotional responses. The crucial question for most people is whether anything of the sort is justified by objective conditions in the universe. We may be willing to remain ignorant about the chances of our own immortality, and even about the ultimate fate of whatever we consider to be good. We mainly want to be assured that a controlling power exists in terms of which all things could be explained—if only we had intellects capable of understanding its nature—and that it is purposeful in some manner we might recognize as having consummate value.

✻

By introducing the idea of purpose, we have taken an important step. Life often includes purposes that organize our actions in fixed and sometimes predictable patterns. "Why did the chicken cross the road?" We are expected to find the answer witty because the question has led us to anticipate a motive more interesting than wanting merely to reach the other side. That kind of purpose we take for granted. Life is filled with many like it. But is there one or even several purposes *of* life, over and above the purposes *in* life?

In earlier generations some philosophers believed that the purpose of life is the progressive advancement of the most highly organized species. Others claimed it is just the continuance of life itself. Nowadays one might be tempted to argue that the purpose of life is the replication of DNA. But to each of these replies, we can ask: What is the purpose of *that?* If we say that the final end has no purpose, since it simply *is,* we have concluded that ultimately there is no purpose of life. There would be purposefulness in life, most notably in human life, but no all-embracing purpose for life or being as a whole.

Different as they are, these accounts would seem to share a similar conception of what a purpose is. But that term also needs clarification. There are two primary senses of the word that have been used in Western philosophy. One, which may be considered "idealist," derives from Plato; the other we may call "pragmatic." The idealist sense is best exemplified by Plato's description of creation in the *Timaeus*. He there portrays the world as having been created by a demiurge or Grand Artificer who contemplates the realm of forms and then imposes them, as best he can, upon brute matter. Plato thinks of the forms as eternal possibilities; and he claims that since the Creator is good, he "desired that all things should be good and nothing bad, so far as this was attainable."[5]

Plato formulates this model in order to show how the world may be seen as purposeful. He assumes that the creative agency has in mind not only what is good but also what is best. The Platonic forms are hierarchical, with the Good presiding over all other possibilities as the highest and most desirable object. This doctrine is rationalistic inasmuch as Plato maintains that contemplation employs abstract reason that takes the inquisitive soul beyond the sensory world. In the *Republic*, and elsewhere, he argues that only deductive reason—as in mathematics, logic, and metaphysical intuition—puts us in contact with reality. Only through deductive reason can we envision the ultimate form, which he sometimes calls the Beautiful as well as the Good.

In effect, Plato is saying not only that the world itself is purposeful, but also that activities within the world become more fully purposeful by employing reason and contemplation to realize the best that is attainable. The implications of this approach can be illustrated by touching on a problem in aesthetics. Philosophers have often wondered what is involved in making art. In Plato's view, artistic creativity imitates the action of the demiurge. According to Plato, painters, poets, composers, etc., contemplate a realm of possible forms to which they have access through their powers of abstract reason within the confines of their individual talent. They then impose these forms upon the materials of their art in the hope of achieving a predeterminate good. This good serves as a goal that guides the aesthetic process from its beginnings. Only by recognizing that his initial intuition shows forth reality and the meaning of life, can the artist—or anyone else—pursue the purposes ingredient in human creativity.

Much of Plato's philosophy is magnificent. But there are many difficulties in the conception he offers. They become especially apparent when we remember that in ordinary life, and even (some would say preeminently) in moments of great inspiration, purposefulness does not lend itself to any such analysis. The second approach, which I call "pragmatic," emphasizes the discrepancy between purposive behavior and reliance upon abstract reason of the sort that Plato advocates. Instead of depicting human beings as godlike entities who contemplate eternal possibilities, the pragmatic approach encourages us to study what happens when intelligent animals engage in behavior that we would deem purposive.

Think of a dog, let us say a relatively inexperienced puppy, that has not eaten for some time and presumably feels hunger. Imagine that it can see a bowl of food on the other side of a long chain fence with barbed wire on top. What are the likely events that could reveal the nature of purposive behavior? The dog might leap forward, only to be stopped by the fence. He might try to climb over or dig under it. There may be other unsuccessful experiments. Finally he gets the "idea" or "insight" (both of which I put in quotes because these are phenomena about which we know little or nothing) that leads him to run around the end of the fence. He then eats the food, lies down, and remains quiescent until some later desire stirs him into further activity.

The pragmatic conception interprets purposefulness as part of a process that satisfies organic needs. Purpose consists in appetitive striving that is finally eliminated by the attaining of consummatory goals. During the appetitive phase, the purposive animal undergoes a pattern of trial and error until it manages to get what it wants. Having got it, the animal rests. Its purposefulness is not a function of abstract reason or the contemplation of Platonic forms. It is only the doing of what is necessary to satisfy desires in a systematic, orderly, and therefore "sensible" fashion that happens to work in a given environment.

In books such as *How We Think* and *Logic: The Theory of Inquiry*, John Dewey develops the pragmatic view in great detail and shows its relation to what we normally mean by intelligence. In *Art as Experience* Dewey counters the Platonic approach to creativity by insisting that the ends an artist pursues throughout the making of his object cannot be separated from the means that he employs. Far from being the intuition of a formal and inherently perfect possibility that might have served as a prior goal, artistic effort is a coordinated succession of maneuvers motivated by needs and desires. The process terminates once an acceptable level of relevant satisfaction has been achieved by the artist. His behavior includes appetitive and consummatory phases comparable to what the hungry dog experienced, though far more complex and certainly more conceptual.

Each of these two approaches has its admirers and its critics. We need not adjudicate between them, or even determine whether they may be harmonized in a synthesis that reconciles their differences. The first one needs to overcome skepticism about the faculty of abstract reason that it invokes as an aprioristic attunement to ultimate reality. The second one must justify its claim that even the most elevated of human activities—in art, in ethical conduct, in religion—is based upon motivation similar to what occurs in animal behavior directed toward the satisfaction of organic needs. Of more immediate importance is the possibility that neither view of human purpose and its sources elucidates a meaning of life. Each may only make sense as an account of purposefulness *in* life. Examples of appetitive behavior and abstract reasoning abound. They are readily observed, though philosophers differ greatly in their theorizing about them. But what are we to say about extrapolations to the entire universe?

✳

If we follow Dewey, we are likely to end up with a materialism that sees the cosmos as a field of contending forces in which purpose exists only to the extent that conscious creatures strive to gratify their own interests. If we follow Plato, we ascribe to some divinity or universal being a concern for higher values that humanity may pursue in an attempt to rise above its mundane condition.

In various ways, philosophers have tried to undermine suggestions that there might be this kind of superior purpose. For instance, if we said that a demiurge or a God of the Judaeo-Christian variety created the world in order to bring about as much goodness as possible, would we not be involving ourselves in an infinite regress? For we should have to ask whether God's purposiveness was itself occasioned by a prior purpose. It is not self-evident that a Supreme Creator must want to maximize goodness. If that desire is ascribed to his "essence," we might still wonder whether such an essence manifests some further, more ultimate purposefulness. We may have made an advance in seeking for the meaning of life, but the quest will have shown itself to be endless.[6] Nor will we have made much progress if, in the pragmatic mode, we suggest that everything seeks its own completion as if it were all part of a cosmic organism trying to satisfy its natural appetites. For then, too, we awaken questions about the purposefulness of that animate totality.

Some philosophers argue that if there were indeed a comprehensive purpose of life, that alone would deprive us of traits human beings have always valued and sought to preserve. We pride ourselves on being free and autonomous, capable of heroic achievements when we live in accordance with our ideals. If, however, we are constituents of a cosmos that has been designed to fulfill a purpose, our status does not differ greatly from that of a tool or instrument fashioned with a predetermined end in mind. The form and use of a kitchen utensil is defined by the function it was designed to carry out. If humanity, or life in general, was created to serve a purpose beyond itself, our being would be analogous to that of a manufactured artifact. There seems to be little in this state of affairs to justify the exultation that religious people sometimes feel in thinking that God's plan reveals the purpose and the meaning of all reality.[7]

Within the linguistic orientation that has characterized much of contemporary philosophy, queries about life's purpose are often rejected in a more radical manner. We are encouraged to believe that such language may really be nonsensical. In order to have meaning, our remarks must have a logical form that is syntactically and semantically adequate for expressing a meaningful question.

We assume that a sentence such as "What is the purpose of life?" makes sense because it has the same grammatical form as sentences like "What is the purpose of pre-heating the oven?" This question is intelligible and has relevance to an observable purpose in life. But though the first utterance has a similar *grammatical* structure, there is no assurance that it has any meaning whatsoever.

To see how we might be fooled in this respect, compare the following sentences: "When it is 5 p.m. in New York, what time is it in Los Angeles?"; "When it is 5 p.m. in New York, what time is it on the sun?" Since clock-time is defined in terms of the angle at which the sun's rays strike some location on the earth, the second of these sentences is nonsense. Whatever its pretensions, a question about time on the sun is internally inconsistent. It has no coherent logical form, and is therefore not really a question. To take it seriously is to waste one's energy. Should we not say the same about putative questions about the purpose of life? Despite the beguiling arrangement of their grammar, are they not equally nonsensical?

This linguistic argument seems very powerful to me. We have often observed purposes in the world, and we know what someone asks when he raises questions about a particular pattern of behavior. But though we are immersed in the cosmos, it is not clear that we can have experience of the cosmos as a whole. We cannot stand back and regard the universe in its totality, as we might do with one or another of its parts. We have no awareness of a second universe with which to compare our own. For the most part, our language is a function of what we can experience or imagine on the basis of experience. We participate in life; we experience it directly; and that can give us knowledge of the purposes within it. But if these purposes must be grounded in a larger purpose that underlies the entire universe, nothing that we try to say or ask about the meaning of it all may really make sense.

And yet, questions about the purpose or meaning of life are not necessarily self-contradictory, or inconsistent, like questions about time on the sun. They are certainly vague, and must always involve perilous extensions beyond ordinary experience. They must be treated as metaphoric and symbolic rather than literal or factual. But this alone does not deprive them of intelligibility. It merely puts them in a category that is closer to poetry than to science. This need not be a serious impediment. Our linguistic capabilities are infinitely diverse. Though there may be good reasons for renouncing the quest for a meaning of life, we should not dismiss such interests merely because they require a language that is hard to understand.[8]

✳

If our concern about the meaning of everything cannot be rejected in advance, on purely linguistic grounds, theories about what that meaning might be are worth studying. Traditional Western religions trace it to an entity they call *super*natural because it exists apart from space, time, and all other coordinates of nature. This Being has a plan in accordance with which he (in the usual ascription of gender) has created the universe. Moreover, he has given everything the ability to live in accordance with his design. The cosmic plan, together with this innate capacity, provides an underlying purpose such that once we understand it we perceive the meaning of life. Millions of people have accepted that account as persuasive and reassuring, a fount of spiritual sustenance throughout their lives. How can this system of beliefs be rejected as nonsensical or logically inadequate?

To begin with, one would want to know what is meant by a universal "plan." Is it similar to the blueprint that an architect draws up before building a house? God, or whatever we call the supernatural being that establishes the purpose of life, presumably creates the universe in an attempt to carry out his prior design. All of nature strives to accomplish his intention, and we may liken this to construction workers following the architect's blueprint. But to talk in this way is to assume that one can refer to an intentionality *outside* of time and space comparable to what occurs within. That is the basic flaw in the analogy.

What can it mean to assert that something is "outside" of time and space? We might argue that numbers exist apart from time and space; and if someone were to claim that for all eternity $2 + 2 = 4$, we would know what is being said. But we would never suggest that numbers have the same properties as things *in* time and space. We do not say that numbers come into or go out of existence. We may even deny that they exist at all. We certainly do not believe that their relationships reveal a "purpose." In talking about a purposive being whose creativity gives value and a goal to all existence, it is as if Western religions confused abstract entities, such as numbers, with things in time and space. It is not a question of determining whether we can fathom the cosmic plan, or prove that a cosmic-planner exists, or manage to fulfill his purposive program. It is a question of knowing whether our mind is able to formulate these notions with any degree of clarity.

One's motive for seeking a meaning of life is quite evident. The problems of living would be greatly simplified if everything could be shown to make sense in terms of a goal toward which it was or ought to be tending. Even if this goal was inescapable or predetermined, we could still acquiesce and happily perform whatever actions are required. Of course we might also conclude that since all decisions must somehow follow the ineluctable order of things, it does not matter what we choose. Some might find this liberating, others might deem it injurious to their sense of freedom; but everyone could feel that an objective explanation has been discovered. Whatever the emotional response, the power of the human mind would at least have been established. Our species would have proved its ability to solve the greatest of all puzzles.

In the history of ideas, many great philosophers (beginning with Plato and Aristotle) have defended the belief in an Ultimate Being or Highest Good that provides objective ends each thing or person must pursue in order to fulfill itself. In theology equally great thinkers, such as Aquinas, have tried to codify our intuitions about the supernatural. This is not the place to engage them in debate. Instead I suggest, as others have in the last two hundred years, that such concepts issue from our human attempt to magnify and idealize what is merely natural. Far from transcending nature, we glorify the aspects that matter to us. In the process we both aggrandize our imagination and inflate our own experience.

Human beings seek a prior meaning in everything as a defense against doubts about the importance of anything, including man's existence. Though we see people expend a great deal of energy on matters of personal concern, we are also aware of human limitations. We know that we are mortal, living for fairly short periods, and that nothing we may do or feel can have a major influence upon the universe. There appears to be a disproportion between the seriousness with which men and women approach their multiple interests and the relative insignificance of these interests within the cosmos as a whole. If, however, the world itself pursues a goal toward which we all contribute, this basic disproportion would be resolved. What matters to us surely does matter if the course of reality includes it within some truly objective design. To affirm that there is a supreme meaning of life is to give the intellect an opportunity to escape the disquieting conclusion that *nothing* people do can possibly have more than slight importance.

The belief that human purposiveness has no real significance belongs to the philosophical view called "nihilism." This, in turn, is related to the idea that our existence is inherently "absurd." The beginnings of absurdist thought may be traced to David Hume. He argues that there is no knowable true statement from which one can deduce the existence of anything (except in a tautologous fashion). In other words, as far as we can tell, everything that is exists for no necessary reason. Hume reached this conclusion because he thought that causality is always ascribed to events that occur in a regular but ultimately arbitrary fashion. Every existing entity is just a *surd*—its occurrence is not necessitated by anything else even though it appears in a constant sequence with events that precede or follow it.

From this, one may conclude that there is no meaning of life, only a pervasive complex of basically inexplicable structures.

Objects and events just happen to be as they are. There is no inherent reason for them to be or not to be, even though our minds become habituated to their usual appearance. They are not planned in any objective sense, and their existence cannot be explained by reference to a prior being.

In books such as *Nausea* and *Being and Nothingness*, Jean-Paul Sartre uses Hume's idea to express the nature of all factuality. Nothing that exists, he says, has any ontological necessity requiring it to be; and therefore its existence can never be "justified" or shown to be required for the existence of anything else. That is what Sartre means when he postulates the "contingency" of everything human, and of being in general. Since I am contingent, nothing fundamental in the world would be different if I did not exist. There may be interesting existential consequences of my never having been—for instance, my children would never have existed—but such considerations are irrelevant, since my children cannot be justified either. They exist, if they happen to do so, only as haphazard occurrences and not as the exemplars of an ultimate meaning in the universe.

In the writings of Albert Camus similar ideas about the absurdity of life are extended in a way that is especially pertinent to our discussion. Camus focuses upon the discrepancy between man's "longing for happiness and for reason" and his inevitable awareness that there is nothing in the universe to satisfy this longing except in a meager or ephemeral manner. The cosmos does not care about human welfare. Camus remarks that "the absurd is born of this confrontation between the human need and the unreasonable silence of the world."[9] It is as if the life of every human being, from beginning to end, was simply a ridiculous rearranging of the chairs in the dining room of the *Titanic* after it has hit the iceberg. For us the iceberg is our finitude, our mortality, and the absurdity of our life lies in our inability either to forgo our customary strivings or to ignore the fact that reality shows no interest in dignifying and preserving them.

Developing a related theory of the absurd, Thomas Nagel says it results from an opposition between what he calls man's "self-consciousness" and his "self-transcendence." He means that the seriousness with which human beings live their lives conflicts with their capacity to transcend this attitude by seeing themselves as "arbitrary, idiosyncratic, highly specific occupants of the world, one of countless possible forms of life."[10] The absurd arises from a discrepancy between our inclination to take our values seriously, as if they were really important, and our awareness that nothing in the universe justifies their existence. Like Camus, Nagel concludes that ultimately and objectively there is no basis for believing that anything matters.

In proposing their conceptions of absurdity, these philosophers assume a contradiction, or at least a split, between man and the world, and also between two aspects of human nature. Man is portrayed as inherently divided between his purposive desire to pursue whatever goals he values and his being as a self-transcending spectator who recognizes that the world is wholly unresponsive either to him or to his values. The world does not seem to mind destroying, sooner or later, everything man cares about. His sense of absurdity is therefore a painful counterpart to the intellect's demonstration of human pretentiousness.

Is this line of reasoning really cogent? For one thing, it is hard to imagine where the "serious" side of man could have come from if there is nothing to maintain it. Thinkers like Sartre and Martin Heidegger defend the absurdist approach by arguing that human life is predicated upon nothingness inasmuch as nothing has value or meaning until man brings these categories into existence. Strictly speaking, that is not correct, as these writers also perceive on occasion. For everything a sentient being wants will be valuable and meaningful to it, to some extent at least. This holds for all creatures that are able to have desires, even if it is true that only human beings can formulate the *concept* of value or meaning. In any event, it does not follow that values issue out of nothing or that the world does not sustain them.

What is meaningful to a human being originates in the vital necessities of the human condition, and that results from nature as it exists in us. It would indeed be absurd to expect inanimate objects or beings in some remote galaxy to share our own system of values. Human beings belong to nature in ways that are defined by the evolution of life on this particular planet. The seriousness of man does not *contradict* the world but rather springs from it as a new but wholly compatible expression of phenomena that may or may not occur elsewhere.

To assert that human interests are always pretentious or disproportionate, and therefore absurd, is to use a metaphor that does not apply. Rearranging the chairs on the *Titanic* is absurd because one then acts as if there is reason to prepare the dining room for passengers who will notice the placement of furniture, whereas everyone has already begun to scurry for the lifeboats. It is likewise absurd—to use one of Camus' examples—for an individual armed with nothing but a sword to attack machine guns, since the man who makes the attempt must know (as we do) that it cannot succeed. But one who tries to live a meaningful life does not manifest a similar confusion. He is not necessarily assuming that his values matter to the universe at large. He may act as he does with full recognition of the context in which he acts. Though the meaningfulness of his existence may be shortlived or highly circumscribed, that need not doom his efforts to futility. To say that one's interests are absurd would be to claim that here, as in the case of the *Titanic* or the solitary swordsman, one's knowledge about reality inevitably contradicts the gamut of beliefs implied by one's behavior. That claim seems to me wholly unwarranted. What could be the content of these damaging beliefs? An assumption that one's values are preordained or that one's life will go on forever? Or that it may consist of unalloyed pleasure, infinite achievement, increasing fervor, and continuous onward momentum? Sometimes people do act as if this is what they believe. But even so, the question remains: Does the pursuit of meaning *presuppose* such ideas? There is no reason to think that it does.

Since the absurdist philosophers assert that values issue from nothing and that the world therefore provides no ground for meaning, it seems strange from the very outset that they should consider man's condition to be inherently absurd. For that implies there is some other way for human beings to exist, though they absurdly fail to do so. But if there is no such alternative, as these philosophers insist, the concept of absurdity cannot be relevant to actual existence. I am willing to agree that men and women often yearn for unattainable goals, and that this sort of attitude may well be called absurd. But why should *all* human striving be characterized that way?

The absurdist philosophers observe, or assume, that the universe has no overarching purpose and, apparently, no concern for human welfare. Since people nevertheless continue to pursue cherished goals, the philosophers see a contradiction between the purposefulness in man's struggle for life and the general purposelessness of the cosmos. This is what they consider the source of human absurdity. I have been arguing that no contradiction, and therefore no absurdity, can be derived from the stated facts. If someone does think that his values matter to some ultimate being, while deep down he knows this cannot be true, his attitude reveals an obvious inconsistency that may justify calling it absurd. But the absurdists are unable to show that our pursuit of goals must always involve this type of contradiction. On the contrary, they themselves usually exhort us to live in a purposive manner that will be free of delusive hopes about corroboration from the universe. They call this an acceptance of our basic absurdity, but it would be more correct to say that acting for realistic goals without harboring false expectations means *avoiding* the alleged contradiction. If we do that, our life is not absurd. Since the absurdists believe that man can follow their recommendations, they cannot cogently argue that his condition is absurd by its very nature.

At this point we may reconsider motives that drive us to ask for the meaning of life. As a purely practical matter, would we not reduce the agony of our existence if we were certain that we are instruments in a grand and purposive design? Alone and afraid in a world we never made, we often yearn for marching orders from a superior power whose greater authority will direct our energies while making us feel sure that they are being properly used. And if we believed in such a power, would that not absolve us of absurdity?

Many people have said that it would, and have claimed that it does in their case. They must nevertheless confront the problem of validation. If a voice from the clouds suddenly booms forth instructions about how we should live, we must still determine that we are not having an auditory hallucination. And if we are told to act contrary to our own deepest feelings and intuitions, are we really obligated to accept the dictates of the superior being? Even if we acquiesce, what have we learned about the meaning of life? Submission to the higher power might simplify our lives and even help us go on living, but in itself it would not indicate what the meaning of life is. For we would still need to know why the words of this individual must be taken as the ultimate authority. Perhaps it gets its own sense of importance by arbitrarily giving orders to inferior beings. Perhaps it is carrying out the commands of a power higher than itself, even though reality as a whole has no meaning whatsoever.

One might reply that having access to vividly articulated prescriptions for behavior is so great a joy that we should not care about their final validation. That makes sense. But if we do not really care about final validation, then neither are we seeking a meaning of life in any objective sense. Instead we will have subtly redirected our original investigation. Rather than searching for a prior meaning of life, we would be asking what is needed for someone to have *a meaningful life*. This is a different kind of question: it orients us toward possibilities that emanate from man's estate regardless of any external meaning that may or may not surround it. Even if there is no meaning of life, or if this meaning is unknowable, or if the entire question is nonsensical in some respect, we may nevertheless hope for illumination about the circumstances under which human beings are able to achieve a meaningful existence.

Though Camus and the others say the human condition is absurd, they establish only that men and women act as if they can have meaningful lives while also believing that the universe does not give a damn. And if people act this way, are they not creating values and a meaning for themselves? The absurdists might agree. But in thinking that all human interests are merely arbitrary, all equally absurd, they cannot explain why people do (or should) prefer any particular attitude toward man's inescapable absurdity. Suggesting irony as an appropriate response, Nagel says: "If *sub specie aeternitatis* there is no reason to believe that anything matters, then that does not matter either, and we can approach our absurd lives with irony instead of heroism or despair."[11] But Nagel is obviously advocating, or at least favoring, irony as a suitable and meaningful reaction, just as Camus had proposed heroic defiance as the means by which human beings can overcome the absurdity in life. To say anything of this sort, however, is to admit that human existence is not wholly absurd. It then behooves us to determine the nature of meaningfulness and how it may be attained.

In a recent book, Nagel suggests that the conflict between self-consciousness and self-transcendence can possibly be minimized. He is not sanguine about this prospect, however. He concludes that "the possibilities for most of us are limited," and indeed that it is "better to be simultaneously engaged and detached, and therefore absurd, for this is the opposite of self-denial and the result of full awareness."[12] But once we realize that life is not absurd, since we are able to create meaning in it, we see that Nagel's dichotomies are untenable. Values do not exist *sub specie aeternitatis;* but neither are they merely arbitrary, as Nagel seems to think.

The basic error in the absurdist approach consists in a kind of fallacy of abstraction through which these theorists observe the human condition. Though they realize that people constantly pursue values and construct ideals, the absurdists examine man's experience out of context. They ignore the ways in which our species is always acting as a part of nature. Men and women have the goals and purposes that are meaningful to them because a biological structure in their needs and satisfactions underlies, either directly or indirectly, their creation of meaning. It is not at

all absurd that human beings have the values that they do. These
belong to us as just the natural entities that we happen to be.

Nor is it absurd that we have values that are distinct from
those of a fish or a bird or any other species significantly different
from our own. Each set of values arises out of material and social
circumstances that make an organism to be as it is, which is to say,
as it has evolved in nature. When natural preconditions are
satisfied, the organism is rewarded by consummations that rein-
force a viable mode of living. That is how our values come into
being. That is the soil in which a meaningful life originates.

There is a sense in which the evolution of species may be
considered arbitrary, for we can imagine a world in which
everything could have developed differently. In that sense, nothing
in life is objectively necessary. But in the reality that we know—
nature as it exists, species having evolved as they did—it is not at
all absurd that human beings should seek the values and create the
meanings that they do. This aspect of our being is no less natural
than everything else that constitutes our fundamental humanity.

✳

Thus far I have been discussing two approaches to the
meaning of life: the traditionalist, which includes most of religious
belief in the West, and the absurdist or nihilist. Despite the
differences between them, they are alike in one crucial respect.
Each addresses questions about the meaning of life as if it were a
single something, and moreover, something *findable*. Though their
answers to these questions are diametrically opposed, both approaches look for a unitary, all-embracing set of answers that
somehow might be *there*, waiting to be revealed. The traditionalists
would seem to see the world as a quasi-mathematical problem for
which there must be a definite solution. If we can only refine our
reasoning powers or cleanse our hearts, they say, we are sure to
discover what we seek. Against this optimistic view, the absurdists
despair of ever succeeding in such a quest. They conceive of the
philosophical problem in similar terms, but they believe it is
resolved only by the honest recognition that there is no meaning of

life. The tragedy of man's condition thus consists in his having the propensity to act as if he had found a prior meaning that ratifies his decisions while all the time he senses at the deepest level of his being that no such meaning exists.

But are we sure that we even know what such a meaning could actually be? If we say that the world is or resembles a soluble problem, we use an analogy that may be wholly inappropriate. We have no acquaintance with different universes, as we do with different problems in mathematics, some of which can be solved while others cannot. To *ask* about a meaning of life that we might discover is not nonsensical. We may understand how the human imagination is operating when it poses such questions. To answer them in the manner of the traditionalists or the absurdists is fruitless, however, for they offer no way of verifying that a universe such as ours does or does not have an independent meaning capable of being found. How could we justify or defeat either assumption? What would count as evidence for or against it?

Whether or not the universe has a meaning to be found, the world as we know it is clearly one in which meaning *comes into being*. We frequently observe meaning being created, whether or not these new creations conform to a further meaning that precedes them. Rather than asking for the meaning of life as if it were a single or comprehensive pattern that permeates all existence a priori, we do better to investigate how it is that life acquires or may be *given* a meaning. This meaning is generally ambiguous, as Simone de Beauvoir argues in her book *The Ethics of Ambiguity*. Criticizing the absurdists, she states: "To declare that existence is absurd is to deny that it can ever be given a meaning." Beauvoir prefers the idea of ambiguity because "to say that it [existence] is ambiguous is to assert that its meaning is never fixed, that it must be constantly won."[13] In other words, ours is not an absurd existence in which we seek for absolute meaning although we are convinced that the universe does not afford any such thing. Rather we are creatures who create meaning for ourselves without having objective and unambiguous criteria by which to determine how we should do so.

We therefore need to examine the conditions under which human beings, and other organisms, make life meaningful. To the extent that life becomes meaningful in this accumulative way, its total meaning is increased. This is something we can verify by reference to empirical data. And indeed, when people ask about "the meaning of life," it is often meaning as a developmental phenomenon in nature that really interests them more than anything else.

With this in mind, we can make an additional response to the pessimistic comment of Freud's referred to earlier. We may now say that there is nothing inherently sick about asking for a meaning of life, provided one recognizes that apart from such considerations life is and can be meaningful in itself. If, however, the metaphysical musings arise out of despair that anything man does will ever give sense or value to life, the pathological implications are obvious. The same applies to doubts that we might have about our individual ability to attain a meaningful life. If we function as healthy beings, we act with assurance that people like ourselves are capable of creating sense and value in their lives. To the extent that they do so they augment the meaning of life in ways that would not have existed otherwise. Without meaning of this sort, human existence degenerates into misery and general chaos.

As a variation on this idea, one might say that life itself includes the creation of meaning and value as part of its innate structure. In accordance with the parameters of their individual natures, different organisms—above all, different animals— manifest indigenous modes of meaning without which they could not survive. If a human being asks for the sense or value of his life, he is either revealing uncertainty about which mode is suitable to himself, or else speculating about further ways of achieving a meaningful life. That can be painful, but our species creates meaning by undergoing this dialectic of doubt and innovation. It is by immersing ourselves in "the destructive element"—as Joseph Conrad said—that we are able to have meaning in life.

We must therefore rephrase the usual questions. Instead of seeking the meaning of life as if it were something preexisting, we must study the natural history of mental acts and bodily responses that enable organisms such as ours to fabricate meaning for themselves. We speak of "finding" a life that is meaningful, but the meaning is something we create. Whether or not we believe there is a prior system of intentions built into reality, we need to ask questions of a different sort: How do we actually create meaning? What is the phenomenology of a meaningful life? What will give a meaning to *my* life? Is life worthwhile? Is it worth living? What makes a life significant? Does anything really matter? Can one learn how to live? If so, how does one do it?

I shall return to these questions, but here I would like to linger on the last one. It appeared most graphically in Tolstoy's account of his midlife crisis and subsequent discovery of faith. Tolstoy achieved his own salvation by observing how the peasants lived. Being close to nature and relatively exempt from the depravities of modern society, they seemed to have acquired what he had missed—the intuitive knowledge of how to live. In their case this meant minimal expectation, simplicity of heart, a curtailing of personal arrogance, and spontaneous submission to their lot as human beings. These were the attitudes Tolstoy considered essential for the faith that gives meaning to life.

Other thinkers have offered their own guides to a meaningful existence: the cultivation of creativity itself, aesthetic contemplation, the pursuit of spiritual or humanitarian ideals, the full employment of one's energies, the realization of individual talents, the search for truth, the experience of love in one or another of its modalities.

However we finally analyze these alternatives, they all belong to a spectrum of life attaining meaning it does not have until we bestow that meaning upon it. I refer to the human race, of course, but not exclusively. In most, and possibly all, forms of life meaning arises from the more or less creative response of a particular organism to its environment. Since the environment may include another bit of life, the creation of meaning can be a reaction to what is meaningful in someone else. My attitude means a great deal to my dog. He creates this meaning, and thereby augments the meaningfulness of his life, by the value he gives to occurrences that others may not even notice—small gestures of mine or my momentary moods. By cherishing his responsive meaning, I make my own life more meaningful. In general, meaning will always depend on the value-laden behavior that living creatures manifest. Meaning in life is the creating of values in accordance with the needs and inclinations that belong to one's natural condition. Valuation is the making of choices by individuals striving for a meaningful life in nature. The values and meanings that emerge are, in this sense, facts of nature—not at all transcendental, as various metaphysicians have thought.

Nor is there a single pattern of meaning that runs throughout the universe. The values of a bird are not only different from, but also incommensurate with, those of a fish. Though each may overlap with the other, and human meaningfulness can often resemble both, we need not posit a discernible identity that remains constant throughout. Even if each form of life is driven by a desire to survive—or to perpetuate itself in its own being, as Spinoza would say—this alone does not reveal a generic purpose that everything has in common. For that implies the existence of a particular program or underlying meaning that creatures must all have in the act of surviving as they do. We have little reason to think that any such uniformity resides within the endless variety of meaningful events that life comprises. Even if the many types of meaningfulness derive from a quest for gene replication, these types remain infinitely diverse among themselves.

✳

Having recognized the dangers in speculating about a prior meaning of life, we can now focus our discussion on meaningfulness in living things. We may see them as separate units within a diversified class of meaningful lives, and we may possibly assert that the cosmos acquires greater meaning only to the extent that it includes a totality of lives that become increasingly meaningful. We may even conclude that this growth in universal meaning *is* the meaning of life. I shall return to that idea at the end of this book. Here I merely note that our interest in meaningfulness need not culminate in a stultifying positivism.

However we interpret the nature of meaningfulness, we must realize that it is always changing. It alters as living things create their own modes of meaning. We human beings differ from members of other species in our astounding capacity to innovate, to generate new meanings for ourselves. We are not more purposive than other animals, and we frequently seem to be less gifted than they are as far as personal happiness is concerned. Anyone who has ever watched a bird building its nest will agree that it usually goes about its business with a kind of confidence, security, and single-mindedness that is rare in men and women. Doing what comes naturally, animals often appear contented, sometimes even serene. Walt Whitman admired them for that:

> I think I could turn and live with animals, they
> are so placid and self-contain'd,
> I stand and look at them long and long.[14]

But though this conception of animal life may be attractive, these creatures attain their level of fulfillment largely by pursuing routine purposes in much the same way throughout a lifetime and from generation to generation. What is meaningful to them is usually constraining rather than expansive. Their placidity is correlated with a lack of intellect or imagination. They are limited in their ability to entertain novel or alternate meanings. Our species is unique in its great creativity with respect to meaningfulness. Our systems of meaning vary tremendously from moment to moment, from one individual to another, and from society to society. On the one hand, we are quickly bored by older meanings and are constantly trying to replace them with newer ones; on the other hand, we have the power to enrich what is meaningful by fashioning cultural and artistic traditions that may grow and develop for centuries.

What we define as culture or civilization is itself a complex of institutions and customs that enable people to acquire patterns of meaning throughout a historical continuity. Civilization is always conservative inasmuch as the future determines itself by means of responses—many of them habitual—that preserve what was meaningful in the past. But it is also progressive, since it gives the imagination material for extending earlier attitudes through sophisticated reactions that make possible vastly unforeseen and often unforeseeable variations. In general, nothing will survive unless it is revitalized in accordance with what has current meaning. Even the dead hand of the past, as in outmoded customs or bureaucracies, retains its power over the present only by a constantly renewed acquiescence among those who submit to it. This subservience is, paradoxically, part of their search for meaning. That creative venture is the human opportunity. It reveals *our* program: not only to ask for the meaning of life but also to bring it into being in the endless ways that constitute our creativity.

The capacity to create new and greater meaning does not exist without its perils. I shall address this problem further on. But here I can say a little about the factors that threaten meaningfulness. Physical decay and many types of disease, including mental illness, are often unable to diminish it. Indeed, some of the most meaningful lives are lived by persons who undergo severe pathologies of either mind or body. A meaningful life can and often does result from efforts to overcome such impediments. Some philosophers think that death itself is just another impediment, and that we negate it by having lived a life that achieves its proper meaning. Socrates talks this way in Plato's *Phaedo*. I think instead that we must treat death as the great destroyer of meaning since it is the termination of each life in nature. But human beings know that they will die, and this awareness may itself provide a source of meaning for them. Moreover, the death of one person is an occurrence in the lives of those who survive. For them, too, it can take on creative meaning.

What then is the relationship between death and meaningfulness? Is death the meaning of life, as philosophers and theologians have often said? Or is life the meaning of death, in the sense that we can understand mortality only in relation to the facts about our finite being? Once we have analyzed our ideas in this area, we may find that we are better able to approach the many difficult questions about meaning as it exists in human experience.

2.

THE MEANING OF DEATH

People who write about "the meaning of death" often do so in order to impart news of another world beyond our mortal span, a spirit-world or at least a realm that transcends the limitations of nature. Lest anyone be deceived in this respect, I must warn the reader that I have no such tidings to convey. I have nothing to report about a white light at the end of the tunnel that reveals a continuance of life after death. My long-deceased grandmother has never welcomed me with a cup of chicken soup to the land of those who survive their death in some Elysian field. To paraphrase William James, I am only a philosopher, which is to say someone who has been trained to attack all the other philosophers. It is the *concept* of death that primarily interests me. How do we use that word? Just what does it refer to? Is death simply a termination of life, or does it have other meaning as well?

What is philosophically interesting in the idea of death will appear immediately if we contrast it with the concept of *dying*. The two are very different. Dying is a physical and psychological process whose beginning may be subject to interpretation but whose ending clearly occurs when vital activity ceases. Whether dying can be defined more precisely as culminating in the loss of brainwaves or heartbeat, or whatever, is not a matter to concern us here. For regardless of how such important issues are resolved, the fact remains that we can readily understand what is meant by "dying," whereas it is not at all obvious what "death" means. One might assume that each refers to a state of being, death taking place after dying has completed itself. But if death is nothing but a termination, it is not a state of *being*. Strictly speaking, it is not a state at all. What then are we talking about?

We naively speak of "dying" and "death" as if these were ordinary process-product terms. Consider how we talk about sleep. We treat falling asleep as a condition that results in our being asleep. The former is a process and the latter is a product that results from that process. Dying is also a process. But is death a product comparable to being asleep? It would be odd to believe this since the person who is asleep is the same as the one who was falling asleep. But death is not like that. We cannot say that being dead is analogous to being asleep, unless we think that the person who was dying is still the same although he has died, somehow continuing to exist in this new condition which has resulted from the process that brought it about. If, however, one who is dead no longer exists, as most of us believe, death cannot be related to dying in any way that is parallel to the relationship between being asleep and falling asleep. What then do we mean by death? We use the term with great facility but its logic is obscure.

If we keep in mind the differences between death and dying, it may not matter that the language appropriate for one of these concepts sometimes serves metaphorically for the other. More essential is our understanding of what each concept entails. As a way of beginning, let me quote from an essay that George Santayana wrote after reading Freud's book *Beyond the Pleasure Principle*. Freud had suggested that death is the goal of life in the sense that all organisms are programmed with an innate drive toward their own annihilation. Freud thought this drive supplemented, and interacted with, the equally instinctive drive to perpetuate one's life as long as possible. Santayana interprets this to mean that life is, as he entitles the essay, "A Long Way Round to Nirvana." He then says the following:

> That the end of life should be death may sound sad: yet what other end can anything have? The end of an evening party is to go to bed; but its use is to gather congenial people together, that they may pass the time pleasantly. An invitation to the dance is not rendered ironical because the dance cannot last for ever; the youngest of us and the most vigorously wound up, after a few hours, has had enough of sinuous stepping and prancing. The transitoriness of things is essential to their physical being, and not at all sad in itself; it becomes sad by virtue of a sentimental illusion, which makes us imagine that they wish to endure, and that their end is always untimely; but in a healthy nature it is not so. What is truly sad is to have some impulse frustrated in the midst of its career, and robbed of its chosen object; and what is painful is to have an organ lacerated or destroyed when it is still vigorous, and not ready for its natural sleep and dissolution. . . . The point is to have expressed and discharged all that was latent in us; and to this perfect relief various temperaments and various traditions assign different names, calling it having one's day, or doing one's duty, or realising one's ideal, or saving one's soul. The task in any case is definite and imposed on us by nature, whether we recognize it or not; therefore we can make true moral progress or fall into real errors. Wisdom and genius lie in discerning this prescribed task and in doing it readily, cleanly, and without distraction. Folly on the contrary imagines that any scent is worth following, that we have an infinite nature, or no nature in particular, that life begins without obligations and can do business without capital, and that the will is vacuously free, instead of being a specific burden and a tight hereditary knot to be unravelled.[1]

I find much in this statement that is wise and true to reality as I have known it. Though I will discuss further questions that Santayana does not broach, his perspective seems to me wholesome and correct. He sees that death is a function of life, a termination and possibly a completion of events that we recognize to be native to our existence. This view is far superior to ideas, such as those that various religions regularly refurbish, of death as the meaning of life. Religious dogmas assume something of the sort whenever they depict life as a preparation for a future dispensation to which we shall have access only after we have sloughed off our earthly coils. Some sects even accord the moment of death greater importance than any that precedes it, as if the meaning of a person's life could be revealed by how he dies rather than by how he has lived.

While repudiating such conceptions, we may also want to reject Freud's notion that death is an instinctive goal of life. That idea gives death a function in natural processes, but possibly misinterprets what the function is. I shall develop this argument below. But first I want to study what might be called a "non-natural" meaning of death that has had considerable influence in twentieth-century philosophy.

Without having recourse to religious categories of the usual type, Heidegger argues that man's being is inherently, ontologically, a being-toward-death (*Sein zum Tode*).[2] According to Heidegger, human existence is permeated by a realization that it is finite and heading toward nothingness. Our being must therefore involve the anxiety one constantly feels in knowing that one is always subject to death. Heidegger claims that this anxiety is not merely psychological, since if that were the case one simply might or might not have it. Rather, he thinks, it is inseparable from human existence: in one way or another man is always aware of "the possibility of [his own] absolute impossibility." Life not only tends toward death as a goal or terminus, but also death occurs in human beings as a potentiality that is ever-present to us through our constant foreboding of what awaits us at some undetermined moment in the future.

Characterizing the being of man in this fashion, Heidegger distinguishes two types of response to it. Most people deal with death in a manner that he calls "inauthentic." They attempt to forget or ignore their destiny as finite creatures that will eventually be destroyed by death. They think of death as something that happens to other people, or else as a calamity that they need not consider until it occurs at some distant time their imagination cannot fathom. In order to live a life of "authenticity," Heidegger insists, we must confront reality by a continual awareness of our fate. One then accepts it in the sense that one treats death as a necessity and ceases to fabricate fanciful means of trying to deny it. In this act of acceptance Heidegger discerns heroic grandeur or ultimate dignity. By no longer falsifying the character of his own finitude, the authentic person makes a kind of noble acquiescence and even willing choice. He has attained the "freedom-to-die," which is to say, freedom in the face of death.

Heidegger's concept of the inauthentic is illustrated by something that the cartoonist Al Capp once said. He remarked that when he gets up in the morning he immediately turns to the obituaries in the newspapers and studies the ages of those who have died. If their average age is greater than his own, he feels relieved by the fact that he has additional years to live. If the average age is less than his, he is delighted to see that he has passed the danger. (But what if the average is exactly his own age? Does he stay in bed that day, to minimize all risks?) The inauthenticity of the attitude portrayed by Capp's whimsical account consists in its implicit belief that one can so easily escape the anxiety that motivates a person to make such calculations. However comforting they may be, nothing can liberate him from the ever-looming fatality that is inherent in human existence. Since recognition of it belongs to our very being, a refusal to live in accordance with this knowledge must always lead to inauthenticity. The evasive maneuvers need not be as humorous as Capp's, but they are all equally self-deluding.

We can readily see what is valid in Heidegger's conception of authenticity. There is little virtue, and nothing admirable, in deceiving oneself either about one's own mortality or the mortality of others. But Heidegger wants to say something more than this alone. He claims that we are inauthentic unless we treat death as an element in *all* of our experience. Since we know we will die, he asserts, we cannot have an authentic life without constantly attending to that fundamental fact about ourselves. He then concludes that, painful as it sometimes is, ontological anxiety—anxiety about this "ground" of our being—is a necessary part of all authentic existence.[3]

I find Heidegger's analysis unconvincing. It neglects, or understates, much of a contrary nature that also belongs to the human condition. Even an adequate awareness of possible and eventual death will rarely amount to the preoccupation incorporated in his concept of anxiety. Heidegger does not believe that we must brood on our coming demise to the exclusion of everything else, but he does maintain that anxiety about death is ontologically ultimate since it colors and pervades our entire being. To say this, however, is to minimize the role of other coordinates that often dominate our experience and have greater importance. In wishing to live, we take action against our impending doom. We seek to delay annihilation as long as possible, we try to protect others from it, we pursue ideals that cultivate and perfect the possibilities of life, we focus upon the experience of immediate consummations that defy death by their sheer vitality.

In all these ways we manifest a being that is directed not *toward* death but away from it. To this extent, one might define human existence as a "being-to-overcome-death." Though we know that death will triumph in the end, and though we recognize the constant "possibility of impossibility," our being is more fundamentally oriented toward the preserving and maintaining of life than to anxiety about its termination.

In his critique of Heidegger's ideas on death, Sartre raises somewhat different objections. Since Heidegger defines human existence as a being-toward-death, Sartre says, he treats death as if it were a completion of life, as if it were something that life tends toward as a consummatory goal or meaningful outcome. In that event, death would be tantamount to what Sartre calls "a resolved chord at the end of a melody."[4] He considers this notion totally mistaken.

We can easily see what Sartre means. A melody begins at a moment in time just as a life does, and it ends with similar decisiveness. In the case of the melody, a resolving chord has retroactive significance. It suggests the meaning of what has preceded it. In that sense it has a value and musical function at every point in the melody. The question is whether death has any analogous role in the life that it terminates. Heidegger would seem to say it does. Sartre argues that life and death are not related in this way.

In Sartre's view, death is always foreign to life, a curtailment imposed from without. It is like a pair of scissors that snaps a thread. Unless the thread were liable to such snapping, this could not occur. But the action of the scissors results from causes and events that have nothing to do with the inner constitution of the thread. Sartre sees human existence as a succession of projects and projections that consciousness initiates. Death is their termination. It is not the fulfillment of their intention, but rather a final barrier that descends upon them arbitrarily. We may know that we will die *some* day, but our actual death is unpredictable. It can happen at any time, regardless of our expectations.

Sartre gives the example of a man who courageously prepares to die on the scaffold and determines to make a brave appearance at the end in order to round out his life with dignity. This would be comparable to viewing death as the resolving chord. But before the man can be hanged, he dies of influenza. *That* is what life is like, Sartre states, and it shows why death is not a culmination but only an absurd termination. Death is not a part of life: it only supervenes upon it. Death occurs as a foreign agency, and for no reason that reveals the fundamental nature of the life it dispatches.

Sartre concludes that death never defines human existence. An individual's being consists in what is possible to him. But my death is not my possibility, he claims, since it is merely that which eliminates everything that was possible to me. My death is "an always possible nihilation of my possibles which is outside my possibilities."[5] Far from being basic to what I am, my death is never a reality for me. Once I die it becomes a reality for others: the survivors experience it as something that has happened to me. I myself can never have that experience. Even if I imagine what my death will be like, my conception must be inadequate and somewhat inaccurate, if only because there is no way of knowing exactly how my life will end.

Since death is outside of life and serves as nothing but its elimination, Sartre insists that death cannot give meaning to life. "Thus death is never that which gives life its meanings; it is, on the contrary, that which on principle removes all meaning from life. If we must die, then our life has no meaning because its problems receive no solution and because the very meaning of the problems remains undetermined."[6] According to Sartre, life acquires meaning only as long as it freely chooses its possibilities, the values it projects upon the world. They constitute its being and create its meaningfulness out of nothing. Death, like birth, just happens. It is a brute fact imposed upon whatever exists. It cannot confer on life any sort of meaning.

This conclusion may help to free us from Heidegger's approach, but I believe it is equally suspect. In a sense the two views, antithetical as they may seem to be, are unacceptable for similar reasons. Heidegger failed to emphasize that meaningful acts are devices for surmounting death even though we recognize its inevitability. They enable us to overcome death by creating and expressing values that not only manifest life but also further its ongoing existence in ourselves. Every moment of fulfillment or consummation symbolically defeats the idea of death. It is as if our experience proclaimed to the world: "Though I will die, at least I have achieved this much." Through deeds that are humane, artistic, or merely nurturing, the imagination propels us into a time when we will no longer be but whatever we care about will survive and possibly prevail. We know we will die, but we deploy our energies toward possible occurrences that project themselves through life as it continues in the future.

Sartre understands that meaning arises from the projection of these possibilities. He also perceives that they exist within a context of human finitude. His concept of "facticity" codifies the way in which man's freedom is always conditioned by givens such as the materiality of his body and his dependence on events in nature. Death is for Sartre just another facticity, something that merely happens to human beings, and that is why he thinks it removes the possibility of meaning instead of contributing to it. To say this, however, is to ignore the fact that human projects are normally undertaken and pursued with a sense of temporal realities. Whether they are designed to benefit ourselves or others, they are enacted with the awareness that we will not live forever. They derive their meaning not only from the freedom with which they are chosen but also from our knowledge that sooner or later death will cut them short for us. In functioning as the boundary to our being, death signifies that everything we do must be completed within a more or less brief period of time during which we are continually at risk of annihilation.

It is this recognition, operating as a structural element in our creation of meaning, that Sartre neglects. In his ideas about death, as in much of his philosophy, he sets up a highly problematic dualism between life and death, freedom and facticity, consciousness and body, man and nature. In doing so, he misrepresents the ways in which these contraries interpenetrate throughout ordinary experience.

This shortcoming appears most clearly in Sartre's remarks to Simone de Beauvoir about his own imminent death: "It seems to me natural. Natural as opposed to my life as a whole, which has been cultural. It is after all the return to nature and the assertion that I was a part of nature."[7] Moving as these words may be, they nevertheless reveal a great confusion. Sartre wants to say that insofar as his life was cultural, it exceeded the natural forces that would soon bring it to an end. What he disregards, however, is the way in which the cultural derives from the natural, manifesting forces in nature that are needed for its existence, even though the goals of culture can always deviate from its origins. In a sense, Sartre admits as much when he says that the return to nature, through death, is the "assertion" that he was all along a part of nature. But if his life was always part of nature, how can there be a *return* to it when death occurs? In destroying life, death is no more natural than the processes (some of them cultural) that it eradicates.

Neither is it any less natural. In the life of nature, death is an ingredient that we confront throughout our efforts to pursue meaningful projects within the finite circumstances available to us.

When we live with an awareness of the limits death entails and also symbolizes, we begin to feel the wonder in our ability to do anything at all. In view of the littleness of our lives, even our minor achievements may seem grandiose. Accompanied by a realistic sense of mortality, our decisions about how to live take on a meaning they would not otherwise have. When I was a child I used to be thrilled by the words "they died with their boots on"; and though this phrase seems puerile to me now, I still find it meaningful. It conveys the idea of people dying in the midst of a purposive but perilous activity, people becoming heroic by militant involvement in a mission they have chosen even though it may lead to death—a culmination they do not seek but which belongs to the nature of the enterprise.

There is no sense of absurdity or despair in the slogan I have quoted. On the contrary, it expresses a feeling of suitability, even rightness. Living with your boots on, as a soldier does in battle, it is fitting and a kind of achievement that one should die that way. When death comes, it merely validates the risk we ran in creating the project that gave our lives meaning. Death does not always strike in an unforeseen and irrelevant manner, as happens to Sartre's condemned prisoner. Heroes are not always killed by a chance occurrence—the flu epidemic—that mocks all noble aspirations. They sometimes die in a way that affirms the meaningfulness of their courageous behavior.

Thus Heidegger does not sufficiently appreciate the importance of our having a being-to-overcome-death, while Sartre ignores the extent to which the creation of meaning involves an awareness of death as the ending that signifies the finitude in all our projects. Our lives become meaningful in the struggle to defeat death even though we realize that everything we attempt belongs to a natural condition delimited by death. One might say that all human experience is doomed or futile insofar as death will happen regardless of what we do about it. But there is no absurdity or ontological failure in this. It is just a part of our mortality, which is natural to our condition. Though the meanings we create will disappear sooner or later, they further life in the present and prolong it for a while in the future. To that extent they succeed in overcoming death, and they do so in the only way available to creatures such as we.

If this is how we think of death, we will see it as neither the prelude to some glorious hereafter nor as the final chord that imparts a resolution to all that preceded it. But we can still envisage death as an event that may possibly serve as the appropriate and timely completion of the life it terminates. Life and death are both fortuitous in some respects. It is arbitrary, in the sense that it just happens to be the case, that we live in a period of history when warfare or famine or cancer has not yet been conquered and therefore people are prevented from living as long as they someday may. It is always fortuitous that anyone should die when and how he does, since the world could have been such that those particular causes of death might not have existed. But it is not arbitrary or fortuitous that beings like ourselves, who participate in nature as we do, should die at some time and in one way or another.

Partly following Sartre, Thomas Nagel claims that death is an absurdity because, from an individual's "internal" point of view, one's own "existence seems . . . to be a universe of possibilities that stands by itself, and therefore stands in need of nothing else in order to continue."[8] But this is not true to our experience. We generally, and perhaps always, know that our possibilities are inseparable from the limitations indigenous to our being. We can *feel* that we may live forever, as we can imagine anything that is not logically self-contradictory, but that feeling must always be suspect. It is not based on observation, and except in moments of illusion it usually has little effect upon the quality of our consciousness or the decisions that we make.

Most people realize that death is one of the major facts of their life. And when we live our lives with a genuine recognition of this particular fact, acting resolutely in response to it, giving life meaning *because* we know that we will die in the not-too-distant future, death ceases to be a meaningless termination. It will not have solved or resolved anything, but it exists as a constraint that reveals what it is to be alive as human beings are. Acknowledging its presence within the trajectory of our existence can also have a useful consequence. In dilatory creatures such as we, it is possible that nothing much would be accomplished without the awareness that time is bounded for us. Confinement can become creative concentration. As the poet Richard Wilbur puts it, "limitation makes for power: the strength of the genie comes of his being confined in a bottle."[9]

I can illustrate these suggestions, so different from the perspective in either Heidegger or Sartre or Nagel, by the song of Guiderius in Shakespeare's *Cymbeline:*

> Fear no more the heat o' th' sun
> > Nor the furious winter's rages;
> Thou thy worldly task hast done,
> > Home art gone and ta'en thy wages;
> Golden lads and girls all must,
> > As chimney-sweepers, come to dust. (IV, ii)

Shakespeare's lines imply that death can be a meaningful occurrence, not merely ending a life but also effecting a kind of relevant completion. All is not lost if we succeed in doing our "worldly task." It is reassuring to think that life in this world can even be regarded as a task, which is to say, a purposeful activity. The practice that Shakespeare uses for his metaphor—the sweeping of chimneys—satisfies a social need. It is an honorable occupation, and those who perform it may point to the ashen dust in their hair as proof that they have carried out their service. So too may lads and girls, whose hair changes from gold to gray and whose bones turn to dust, undergo death as a natural and correlative result of having lived.

The Shakespearean lines can be taken as meaning that death is a benign outcome, like payment to one who has done his job. Later in the scene death is actually called a "quiet consummation." This may seem to us unjustifiably roseate. The ground in which we are buried may strike us as something less than the home to which the honest laborer goes after his day's work. But even so, the word "home" reverberates with a sense of belonging to a familiar and possibly familial setting. Though we need not consider death a boon or consummation, we eliminate some of its horror if we accept it as the befitting conclusion to a natural process.

Sartre's analysis rules out the idea of any rightness or suitability in death. In proposing a different view, I am not suggesting that death always, or often, occurs as a happy ending. I am not saying that in itself it gives life meaning. I only want to leave open the possibility that we can live in such a way that death has an appropriate, and therefore meaningful, place in our being. The projects that determine human experience can be realistic or unrealistic. When they are realistic, they define themselves in terms of boundaries imposed by the physical and organic determinants of life. They are known to be structured not only by their vital momentum but also by their inherent limitation. For each of us this occurs in death. If we deny it, whether for religious or sentimental reasons, we are out of touch with our own existence. If we accept it as part of what it is to be a human being, we surmount it in advance. Death is incapable of depriving life of "all meaning," as Sartre maintains, if the projects that give a life its meaning are undertaken with a staunch recognition that even at their best they cannot last forever.

Though life begins with birth and ends with death, human consciousness exists in the apparent timelessness of the present moment. It is therefore understandable that conscious beings like ourselves may sometimes feel alienated from their temporal restraints and even consider them an absurdity. But death is not absurd, just as birth is not. Without the latter, we have no existence; and unless technology can radically alter our current state, the same is true of the former. These are elements of our life in nature, regardless of what we might prefer. It would be fanciful, and even irrational, for us to think that we are able to live without dying and yet belong to the same natural order that has created us.

If we choose, we can rebel against our finitude, as Dylan Thomas does in the lines about his father's proximate death: "Do not go gentle into that good night,/Old age should burn and rave at close of day;/Rage, rage against the dying of the light."[10] An old man is less likely to have this attitude than his young son, but the feeling is not inappropriate though possibly unfortunate. Raging against death is hardly the best method for delaying it, and the vehemence of our rejection can prevent us from attaining a meaningful response to the final outcome. I am suggesting that we do so when we accept death, not in the sense of glorifying it or confusing it with a consummatory good but rather in seeing it as one of the coordinates without which we would not exist. Acceptance of this sort is essential if we are to achieve the greatest meaningfulness in our actual condition.[11]

❋

The concept of anxiety that Heidegger and Sartre employ in their attempts to show how man should cope with death is worthy of close attention. I defer that discussion to the following chapter since it is related to questions about the creation of meaning. The fear of death differs from anxiety in being focused on the specific event which is the destruction of life in us. Psychologists, of whom Elisabeth Kübler-Ross is the most renowned, have done excellent work analyzing the stages that people go through in the process of dying. Philosophers have traditionally asked a different kind of question. They have wanted to determine whether it is *rational* to fear death. Some have thought that we might be cured of our fear if only we recognized that this feeling—unlike many others— cannot be justified by reason. It would be rational, for instance, to fear something that we know to be harmful. But if being dead is unknowable or a state of nothingness, we need not assume that it does us any harm. One could then conclude that there is no rational basis for dreading it. Once people realize this, will they not be able to control or even exorcise their painful fear?

Idealist philosophers have often argued against the fear of death by claiming that our little life is not rounded by a sleep but rather encased in a meaningful universe that transmutes death into a beneficial event we should gladly welcome. Arguments of this sort appear in Plato's *Apology* and Hegel's *Lectures on the Philosophy of Religion,* among many other philosophical works. It is more pertinent, however, to consider the beliefs of philosophers who treat death as a total, irreversible destruction of each individual and yet who claim it is not rational to fear it.

The most famous argument along these lines is the one that Epicurus offered in ancient Greece. Epicurus said: When we are, death is not; when death is, we are not; therefore, it is irrational to fear death. Epicurus was addressing people who worried about punishments they might receive in an afterlife that traditional religions have often portrayed. Having rejected faith in any such immortality, Epicurus could take comfort in the belief that there is no possibility of retribution beyond death. And to those who may have feared death because they thought they would suffer after dying, his reasoning may well have been persuasive. But it scarcely deals with the problem of most people nowadays, who are not apprehensive about hellfire but who are afraid that they will be annihilated by death. What they fear is precisely the circumstance Epicurus specifies: that they will not be when death is.

In other words, Epicurus' slogan fails to show that the fear of death is irrational in those who fear they may be terminated completely. To tell them they will be nothing after death and thus there is nothing to be feared is simply unhelpful. The feeling of dread, which Epicurus was trying to alleviate, is often very strong, and if it is to be deemed irrational, this must be demonstrated by a more sophisticated argument.

In that attempt Lucretius suggested the following: Life is a finite span from birth to death; before birth there was an infinity of nothingness out of which we arose, and after death there will be an infinity of the same kind; it would never occur to us to fear or bewail our not having existed during all those eons that preceded our birth; therefore there is no reason why we should fear the comparable non-existence that will ensue after death. Lucretius assumes, of course, that if it is irrational to fear some particular state of affairs, it is equally irrational to fear one that is equivalent or very similar.

Lucretius is right in thinking that we would consider it irrational to have fears about non-existence prior to our birth (though we might regret and even lament that we were not alive during the heyday of Greek culture, or the Renaissance, or some other era). But he is mistaken in thinking that our fear of death is at all comparable. Before we were born, we did not exist and therefore had nothing to lose. We fear death because we fear the loss of life, much as a mother fears the loss of her child, or a lover the loss of his sweetheart, or a miser the loss of his money. In each case people fear that they will be deprived of a good they possess. And can anything be more clearly good than life itself—at least, for one who enjoys his existence and appreciates the many satisfactions that belong to a life worth living? For such a person, the fear of death would seem to be supremely rational.

The patriot who dies for his country and the revolutionary who dies for the cause he believes in may say they fear death less than they fear betraying their ideals. This attitude does not prove it is irrational to fear losing one's life, but only that devotion such as theirs can lead a person to make enormous sacrifices for something he cares about. Dedicating ourselves entirely, we may even find that our fear of death has disappeared. This, however, does not mean that the earlier fear was irrational. Nor can Lucretius' argument be salvaged by anything else that motivates our willingness to return to the non-existence that preceded birth. It is always rational to want to retain whatever life we have and value. The situation is not the same, or in any way equivalent, before we have it.[12]

In Schopenhauer's conception of death we find a very different type of argument. People fear death, Schopenhauer says, because they think of themselves as separate substances, each unique and ontologically independent. This is erroneous, he insists, since we—and everything else that lives—are but manifestations of an ultimate metaphysical force that courses through all of nature. This force, which follows deterministic laws and in itself has no purpose, is "the will." As we saw, he uses that term to characterize the underlying reality because he thinks we come closest to intuiting its presence through our volitional and instinctual being, which includes our sexuality. The will is a will to live; it shows itself primarily as a striving for its own preservation. Since intellect is useful for the perpetuation of life, it has successfully evolved in man. To the extent that it furthers survival, the intellect serves the will and remains congruent with reality. But no sooner does intellect come into existence, Schopenhauer states, than the will has difficulty controlling it. The idea that human beings are separate from the rest of nature and have independent lives whose individual destruction is a calamity—all this bespeaks the waywardness of intellect.

We *are* the will, Schopenhauer claims: our life is only an expression of it. When we die, our personal energies are merely reprocessed by the cosmic force that has briefly appeared in us and will now appear in something else. From this point of view, death does not destroy our individuality, since we never really had it in the first place. Death is a transitional moment of no great consequence to the will. The intellect gives death undue importance and that is what generates our fear. The fear of death must be irrational because it is based upon a fallacy. Far from being negative or undesirable, death serves to eradicate delusion. It removes a misconception—the idea of our individual substance—that the intellect has foolishly instilled. Since the will survives and since we are nothing but local manifestations of it, there is no reason to dread its transfer into other entities. That is all that happens when we die.

Without examining the problems that belong to metaphysical theories like Schopenhauer's, I shall only point out one obvious flaw in his doctrine. Schopenhauer says it is irrational to fear death since this emotion issues from the intellect's delusions about our separate being. But even if this is true, the fact remains that humans are what they are partly *because* of their intellect. Even if we are exchangeable and expendable parts of an impersonal force in nature, our actual experience of ourselves is nothing like that. We exist in the world as individuals, as beings whose consciousness and self-awareness are unique to each person in his or her particularity. We are living nodules that may intermesh with one another but never lose all vestige of delimiting differentiation. If we had no intellect and our experience were other than it is, we might have no sense of independent being. But since we have this, and only this, way of living—even though Schopenhauer's own intellect questions the reliability of intellect in general—it is not surprising that we should feel great apprehension about whatever eliminates the condition we recognize as our own. Radically deluded though we may be, thanks to the metaphysical errors of the intellect, that is what we *are* by our very nature. Consequently, it seems perfectly rational for us to fear the momentous event that can and will annihilate us.

I conclude that there is no basis for considering it necessarily irrational to fear death. Unless we are convinced that greater benefits will compensate us for the loss of cherished goods enjoyed in the process of living, the fear of death is always rational. I do not mean that this feeling is inevitable or unavoidable; and certainly it is counterproductive when it becomes a painful obsession that interferes with our ability to savor life and go on living. On many occasions the fear of death is needed for self-preservation. Without a salutary fear we might run risks that would markedly decrease our chances for survival. In the long run our gene pool would suffer and the species might even be imperiled. From this we can infer that it is sometimes *desirable* to fear death. That must depend on the consequences in each case, but it does indicate that one can imagine circumstances in which the fear of death would indeed be wholly justified.

In the final analysis we fear death because we love life, at least enough of it and in sufficient degree to believe that our existence is worth continuing. In a vigorous organism both the fear and the love arise from instinctual roots and are often inseparable. To impose criteria of rationality may therefore be considered pointless. But our reason is also part of nature, and it is natural for us to seek some rationality in what we feel. However strong and deep within our psyche, no emotions are self-validating. That is why we cannot say that the fear of death, or even the love of life, *must* be rational—only that it is not inherently irrational.

❇

If it can be rational to fear death, one may nevertheless wonder why that fear is absent in many people whose rationality would never be questioned. I have long thought about the paradoxical fact that, on the whole, young persons fear death more acutely than older ones, even though the latter are statistically closer to their demise. The elderly are no less rational, and they have had greater experience of death as an unwanted intrusion upon the lives of others. Yet they generally suffer much less from the fear of death than they themselves may have done when they were young. In addition, the fear of death is often inversely correlated with the quality of experience and the feeling that one's life has been fairly successful. While they stand to lose more by dying, men and women who are happy or have meaningful lives tend to fear death less than others do. Though the sense of having lived well may enable human beings to face their fate with equanimity, the situation remains anomalous. Where one has access to a greater goodness in life, should one not have greater fear that it will be obliterated by death?

Freud's explanation for this paradox is related to his theory about the "death drive," which he considered innate in everything that lives. His conception is somewhat unclear, but it would seem to take the following form: We all have in us an instinctual need to return to the inorganic state out of which life evolved; this regressive impulse limits the search for new experience and further exploration on the part of our equally instinctual life-force; when people get older, they survive by adjusting to the diminution of energy in themselves as they approach the goal their death drive has been seeking; it is therefore easier for them to become reconciled to the eventuality that appeared so repellent when their vital impulse was both powerful and predominant.

Freud need not be understood as suggesting that all human beings have a *wish* for death. Though he is often misquoted in this fashion, his metaphysical hypotheses—which he himself found puzzling and unverifiable—may be given a more moderate interpretation. Instead of claiming that everyone wants to die, he may only have meant that we possess a basic capacity for accepting death as the programmed goal of life.

If we read Freud this way, we can explain the lessened fear of death in older persons as a constitutional response that appears under suitable circumstances. Though perhaps we should not call it an instinct, the progressive acceptance of death might be considered a potentiality that is biologically determined in all people. As with other biological phenomena, this attitude can also reflect the influence of cultural and individual differences. It may nevertheless occur as a development that is more or less constant in human beings once they reach old age.

Further research may also indicate that the ability to overcome the fear of death increases after one's sexual drive starts dwindling. This could be an evolutionary device related to the utility of discouraging survival among the aging members of a population, whose value for the next generation will have lessened. It might well be the case that our acceptance of death, in the sense that we no longer fear it greatly, is correlated with the decrease in our ability to react quickly and vigorously to anything that threatens the existence of our genetic group. The capacity for immediate responsiveness declines with age, even when the individual's own welfare is at stake. Though many people learn to enjoy life only as they get older—George Bernard Shaw was right when he said that youth is too wonderful to waste on children—the elderly often lose their emotional potency as well as their muscular strength, their sensory acuity, and their intellectual rapidity. In other words, we conquer the fear of death only after our vital forces have been weakened by disabilities and impairments that nature imposes with the passage of time. Death becomes less fearful to us because the energy that enables us to fear anything has been diminished.

Carrying these suggestions a little further, we may posit four or five different stages in our response to death. In the earlier years there is often a narcissistic sense of immortality. The young child acts as if, and in some respects believes that, he will live forever.

Even if he has heard about the death of others, he may have no conception of it as something that could happen to him. He may be afraid that those he loves, and those whose love he depends on, will die or disappear. But that is quite different from the fear of his own death. There is a great variability in the length of time during which this first attitude continues. In children who suffer from illnesses that they know or suspect are terminal, it may be quickly superseded by responses that would otherwise occur much later.

With the onset of puberty, we normally attain the unpleasant realization that death threatens us as it does everyone else. Where the younger child may have played with the idea of being dead, as he also pretends to kill everyone who opposes him, there now arises with vivid consternation the awareness that death will someday strike him down exactly as if he were no different from all other living things that die. Older people often idealize the innocence and boundless vitality of youth. I think they have forgotten how terrifying the first acquaintance with the fear of death can be for many juveniles. Its occurrence partly explains the fascination among the young for horror movies that objectify and express the terror they feel. To some extent, it may also account for much of the violent and troubled behavior that characterizes this period of life. Through a dialectical confusion to which all strong emotions are subject, it may even throw some light on the relative frequency of suicide among adolescents. When it is painful and persistent, the fear of death augments the difficulty of living and thereby makes the prospect of immediate, total escape seem more attractive than before.

Among those who live on, which is to say the vast majority, there generally evolves a slow but gradual acceptance of death as a final termination. This may often take the form of mere adjustment: we become habituated to our fear of death and that makes the idea more tolerable, or at least less terrifying. In either event our mortality tends to become less of a preoccupation than before. We stop feeling the torment that we may have experienced in our earlier years; we become accustomed to the fact that everyone dies, ourselves included. We may still fear death, and to some extent that emotion may be present in all human beings, but it no longer affects us as once it did.

Also, we become used to surviving. We have endured all these years without dying; we have eluded the infinite number of catastrophes that are always possible in life; and so we tend to assume that things will go on the same way. The automobiles that missed hitting us, however barely, will continue to miss us. Illnesses that might have killed us, but didn't, will not kill us when they recur. It becomes easy to believe that we will be able to cope with future calamities as we always have. In a similar vein Mark Twain, when he was almost seventy-five, said that he did not fear death since there were so many catastrophes he had dreaded throughout his life which never materialized. He felt that death, too, would not equal its advance billing.

One should not idealize this stage of life, as optimistic philosophers do when they treat the increased acceptance of death like a blissful twilight that nature offers as a remedy to earlier suffering. In some people this attitude doubtless issues into a period of great peace and serenity; and we may consider that to be an innate capacity in everyone. But in most of us the acceptance of our coming death probably means that we have finally given up trying to unravel ultimate problems and are saving our remaining emotionality for efforts needed to stay alive. Accepting death as an approaching reality may thus signify greater insensitivity on our part rather than profound clarification. It may actually mask a subtle form of inauthenticity. That can be resisted, of course, but it is always possible in human beings.

For many people a further experience follows, or accompanies, the ones I have mentioned. We often transmute the fear of our own death into a greater fear that death may come to those we love. Through love people bestow exceptional value upon other persons and sometimes upon ideals or physical objects. The recipient of our love becomes so intimate a part of our being that the beloved's continued existence may matter to us more than our own. Self-sacrificial love in the saint, the hero, the devoted spouse, the parent defending his or her child is motivated by emotions that frequently include an overwhelming fear of death: not a fear of one's own death, though this may still exist to some degree, but a fear of mortal dangers that can befall the object of one's love.

In the history of ideas, love and death have often been associated with one another. Though a character in Shakespeare claims that "men have died from time to time, and worms have eaten them, but not for love," various traditions in the Western world have maintained that people do die for love and even that love proves itself in the willingness to die for what one loves.[13] In the philosophy of the twentieth-century writer Gabriel Marcel, one finds the suggestion that love is a way of saying to another person that "you shall not die."[14]

If we take this idea literally, it may well seem to be ridiculous. The beloved is just another human being, and nothing we can do will confer immortality. But possibly Marcel means that love is an affirmation of the beloved which bestows endless importance upon that person. In loving someone, an individual encases the beloved in values that may live on after the lovers die. Love includes the hope that their bond will have created a permanent goodness. The lover is telling the beloved: "Even if you died tomorrow, you will survive because our love has been a real and ineradicable achievement in life." That is what T. S. Eliot means when he says, in "A Dedication to My Wife," that neither wind nor sun can kill the roses in the rose-garden which is their love.[15] In this sense love does conquer death.

In sketching these aspects of human development, I am not claiming that they reveal anything like a death-related instinct. On the other hand, they seem to accompany the aging process in ways that are not entirely learned from the environment. We are not taught to fear death acutely in adolescence, or to accept it with forbearance when we get older. Nevertheless, most people do learn how to adapt to physiological and psychological changes that occur throughout the years. One could therefore say that, to some extent, the progressive alteration in our attitude toward death must involve the accretion of learned responses. This does not prevent us from believing that the different stages follow one another in accordance with a complicated pattern that is basically innate. Further evidence may reveal that Freud's speculations, primitive and metaphysical as they were, can have fruitful consequences for research provided they are suitably revised.

For this new research to succeed, it must always recognize that what we mean by death has to be explained in terms of a natural dynamic that constitutes life. There is no meaning of death apart from its meaning in life. Death is so great a problem for human beings only because it intrudes upon our search for a meaningful life. All thinking about death reflects what we consider meaningful to us in life itself.

Our investigation thus takes us back to questions about the nature of meaningfulness. The Japanese novelist Mishima thought that life has meaning only when it is beautiful and therefore, he concluded, one should die before the ugliness of decay sets in. Whether or not he was right, many people have treated the aesthetic as a paradigm of meaning in life. Even if life is sound and fury signifying nothing, as Macbeth thought, it is also a production in which a player "struts and frets his hour upon the stage." But there are different ways of strutting and fretting. And a stage exists within a creative transaction. The player is the embodiment of an art form, and each of his gestures can be meaningful to him as well as to his audience. The question we must now ask is how this (or any other) meaning comes into being.

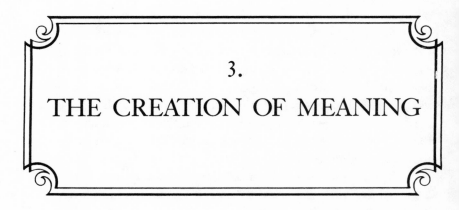

3.

THE CREATION OF MEANING

In this book I have been trying to suggest a naturalistic and empirical approach to questions about life and death. I argued that the meaning of death consists in its relevance to processes within life itself, and I suggested that instead of hoping to find the meaning *of* life we should seek insight into the nature of meaningfulness. Even if we make sense of the idea that there is a single meaning to life, and that this meaning has a prior status that may be discoverable, we still have to determine how life can be meaningful for us.

Those who accept Western religion believe that God's plan provides a foundation for meaning, and we may all agree that their faith simplifies their life by assuring them that everything they do and everything that happens to them is meaningful. But this pattern of belief is based on non-verifiable assumptions that exceed the limits of natural events and ordinary experience. Take away the transcendental props, which nowadays have become wobbly after centuries of criticism, and the grand edifice cannot stand. The challenge in our age is to understand how meaning can be acquired without dubious fantasying beyond the limits of our knowledge.

In "A Brief History of My Opinions" Santayana depicts his struggle with this problem. He describes his boyhood experience as a Catholic who loved what he calls "the Christian epic" but eventually concluded that neither it nor any other cosmic system could be taken as literal truth. "For my own part," he reports, "I was quite sure that life was not worth living; for if religion was false everything was worthless, and almost everything, if religion was true." Looking back at this moment in his life, Santayana interprets his pessimism as the by-product of a conflict within himself between Catholicism and "complete disillusion." He indicates the outcome when he tells us: "I was never afraid of disillusion, and I have chosen it."[1]

Santayana lived a meaningful life. The crisis he portrays frequently occurs among adolescents who come to realize how fragile are the doctrines they have inherited but now find untenable. There is also the sense of disillusionment that often accompanies a child's growing awareness that—like everything else in nature—he too will die. But having found the strength to put aside dogmas he no longer believed, Santayana could then create and carry out projects that were meaningful for others as well as for himself. Though he disintoxicated himself (a term that often appears in his writing) of optimistic assurance that all was for the best, he managed to live a productive and rewarding life.

Santayana's case, like many others, reveals that avoiding the traditional search for meaning need not put us at a disadvantage in our creation of a meaningful life. Though we no longer have authorities whose certitudes can direct us, we acquire the freedom to mold our own destiny. Santayana's approach requires greater courage perhaps, and so it may be harder to attain. But this alone would make it more outstanding as a personal achievement. Nevertheless, Santayana does not explain how his attitude can be distinguished from bravado or mere defiance. For if life is possibly worthless and our values have no objectivity beyond our own decisions, the creating of meaning may be just a superficial display and not especially important. What looks like courage may only be a refusal to accept the bitter consequences of believing that ultimately everything is futile.

This intuition underlies the thinking of Heidegger and Sartre about ontological anxiety. Their concept pertains to the creation of meaning as well as to the nature of death. Heidegger and Sartre assert that death not only issues into nothingness, inasmuch as it terminates life, but also that it symbolizes the inherent nothingness of being. Since the world arises out of nothing and will someday return to it, nothing really matters. They infer that anxiety (as an ontological condition) is the inevitable result of our awareness that nothingness is fundamental in reality. Anxiety is our unavoidable response to the contingency of existence and the lack of final sanction for any ideals or strivings that may guide our behavior. We define ourselves through freely chosen acts, but what we are and what we value must always be predicated on the underlying nullity of everything. Like Heidegger, Sartre maintains that we create meaningful and authentic lives by facing up to this grim fact. But that can happen, they insist, only in the context of ontological anxiety about nothingness.

Neither Heidegger nor Sartre is referring to psychological anxiety. That occurs when we are apprehensive about something in our experience without exactly being aware of what it is. But ontological anxiety is not addressed to anything. It directs itself not to an actual or conceivable something but to the nothing—which is the ground for everything—that Sartre calls "non-being curled at the heart of being."

Unless we can make sense of the notion of absolute nothingness, neither Heidegger's nor Sartre's conception of a meaningful life will be defensible. In a classic article Rudolf Carnap demonstrated the non-sense, the literal nonsense, of treating nothingness in this bizarre and confusing manner.[2] When Heidegger tries to clarify his approach, he admits that there may be no noun that can possibly convey the meaning of nothingness. For every substantival term must deal with a something, while nothingness is the total opposite of that. In his heavy-handed way, Heidegger jokes with the reader. If I am talking about nothing, he says, why should anyone bother with what I have written? Unless I can say something about something, why should anyone read me? He concludes that since there is nothing that *is* nothingness, his meaning can only be conveyed by a verb; and so he remarks that "Das Nichts nichtet." This translates as: "Nothingness nothings."[3]

The move from the noun to the verb cannot extricate Heidegger from his ontological difficulties. One can see why many philosophers who prize honesty of thought refuse to take his effort seriously. It lends itself to parody such as Tom Stoppard's in *Rosencrantz and Guildenstern Are Dead.* In Act III the ship is becalmed that carries the two false friends of Hamlet to England (and to death, though they do not know this). Rosencrantz is bored by their prolonged inactivity. He and Guildenstern have the following conversation:

> *Guil.:* Don't give up, we can't be long now.
> *Ros.:* We might as well be dead. Do you think death could possibly be a boat?
> *Guil.:* No, no, no . . . Death is . . . not. Death isn't. You take my meaning. Death is the ultimate negative. Not-being. You can't not-be on a boat.
> *Ros.:* I've frequently not been on boats.
> *Guil.:* No, no, no—What you've been is not on boats.
> *Ros.:* I wish I was dead.[4]

In part we laugh at this by-play because we feel that critics like Carnap may well be right in arguing that Heideggerian talk about ontological nothingness is nonsensical. We can understand what it is like for something to turn into nothing. First it existed and then it did not. Looking at a computer's monitor, we see a something which is the visual image. Then someone unplugs the machine and we see nothing of the sort. Similar alternations between something and nothing recur throughout our experience. They do not, however, implicate the total and absolute nothingness that Heidegger calls an ultimate ontological category. One might say that his language is poetically metaphoric. That would be acceptable if we could understand his metaphors. I am not convinced that we can. And if we cannot clarify the meaning of nothingness in this special usage, neither will the Heideggerian concept of anxiety function as he would like.

On the other hand, I feel within myself a definite and sympathetic responsiveness to Heidegger's intention, and this feeling cannot be discounted. For if he were merely talking gibberish, how could there be anything in me that resonates to his language? Heidegger is renowned for his claim that the prime question in philosophy is: "Why, in the universe as a whole, is there something rather than nothing?" Heidegger was not the first to have formulated this as a philosophical question. It appears in the writings of Leibniz, in Hume's *Dialogues Concerning Natural Religion*, and much further back in the history of philosophy. If it were a meaningless or nonsensical query, it could not strike us as having real profundity. Yet the question has a strong, albeit ambivalent, effect. Even though I doubt that anything intelligible is being said, I also feel that this is the most important issue that we could possibly consider.

Here again I can illustrate what seems nonsensical by citing a familiar joke. I am thinking of the Jewish story about two old friends who meet after an interval of many years. One asks the other what kind of life he has had. "A very happy one," is the reply: "On the whole, life has been good to me. And you?" "Not bad. I've nothing to complain about. But to tell the truth, if I had it all to do over again, I'd just as soon not have been born at all." "Ah yes," the other sighs, "but who can be so lucky?"

Why do we laugh at this answer? Because it is ontologically paradoxical. In order to exist, one must be born. (The man is not referring to his life as a fetus.) In non-existence there is no capacity for anything. How then could one have been lucky before existing; how could one have "been," whether lucky or otherwise?

If we extend this quandary to the universe as a whole, do we not see the impossibility of trying to conceive of absolute nothing-

ness? And does this not reveal the oddness in asking the philosopher's question about why there is something rather than nothing?
Physicists get into a similar difficulty when they incautiously say
that everything began with the Big Bang and then ask what *preceded*
it. This kind of question does not belong to physics at all,
particularly if one assumes that the physical world originated with
the Big Bang. If there was something before that, it cannot be
understood in the language of physics. If *nothing* preceded the Big
Bang, this too is inexpressible in physics. What then can it mean to
ask what there was before there was anything?

But if the question is truly meaningless, why does it affect us
so powerfully? Why does it constantly hover at the periphery of
consciousness? Why do we feel that in *some* sense we do understand it? Its meaning is perpetually out of reach but almost within
our grasp, like a forgotten name for which we keep groping. I have
no satisfying solution to this dilemma, but I suggest that beyond the
anxiety about nothingness as Heidegger and Sartre use that term
there is an anxiety that must always be more ultimate. This is
anxiety about ourselves as creatures who are able to use language in
so strange and uncertain a fashion. There would be no cause of that
anxiety if we could either understand what is being asked or else
discard such utterances as merely nonsensical. But we seem to be
unable to do either. Nor can we ignore the issue or reject it as a
trivial confusion. We may dismiss the joke about the preferability
of being unborn, but we cannot escape our nagging and disquieting
puzzlement about there being something in the universe rather
than nothing. The anxiety I am describing arises from our
propensity to formulate problematic questions of this sort. It may
not cause distress in everyone, but it lurks within us as a
predicament that is typically human.

This kind of anxiety has a positive as well as a negative aspect.
The positive contributes to the creation of meaning, as I shall
presently show. But the negative warrants further attention. I am
suggesting that it is a radical malaise we feel as thinking beings who
use words that grip us with a sense of great, possibly greatest
importance even though their meaning eludes our comprehension.

This is different from anxiety we might feel in trying to think about a situation that is unknown and even inconceivable. A person might fear death not only because he wants to live but also because he is pained by the fact that he cannot conceive of himself *as dead*. No one can imagine the state of being nothing rather than the something one now is. That is unknowable as well as inconceivable.

Nevertheless, the death of anything, even oneself, is not incomprehensible. We have often seen the termination of life processes. We are very familiar with the fact that events in nature come to an end. I strike a match and thereby ignite a flame. The fire exists by consuming energy. When its material resources are exhausted, it goes out. It would never occur to me to ask where the flame is once it has been extinguished. I understand what is meant by its having existed and now being nothing. In a similar fashion, I may think of my own life as beginning in time, continuing for a while as the flame does, and then disappearing whenever it has used up the matter that was essential for its existence. Though these processes, and the world from which they emerge, are largely unknown and even unknowable to me, I can recognize them as the workings of nature.

My annihilation as the outcome of my having existed may therefore be comprehensible even though the nothingness which results is unimaginable. I cannot know or imagine what it is like to be nothing, but I can understand this eventuality as the terminus of my finite being. What I cannot comprehend is the possibility of *everything* being nothing. One has the feeling that just as some particular flame goes out, so too could *all* flames expire. And if all flames, then why not all things as a whole? And if everything—all matter, all events in the universe, all space and time itself—were to end, each in its own way, would we not have absolute nothingness? One *seems* to understand what is being said. But actually the language defies comprehension. For if there were absolutely nothing, there would be no universe at all. There would just be a void. But what kind of being is *that?* It is not a consistent possibility for us to entertain. It boggles the mind.

This tells us something about our ability to think. It is wholly comprehensible to us that the flame I just ignited should not exist. It is wholly comprehensible that I, or you, or anyone else should not exist. We can surely envisage such possibilities. In doing so, we imagine the universe as it was before, but now deprived of one or another of its former entities. What we cannot comprehend is the universe being deprived of itself. We may *say* that all things can disappear just as any of them might, but the notion stuns and even troubles us. It is as if we were speculating about the end of reality. But it was reality that we were trying to comprehend. How can we do so if we eliminate that concept entirely? We cannot. And yet neither can we avoid having feelings of bafflement and metaphysical discomfort.

Out of this reverberation, obscure as it may be, arises the ontological anxiety that is basic to our condition and that only human beings undergo. It is part of what makes man the sick animal; no other animal suffers from this sickness. To the extent that all people are solipsistic and tend to identify reality with their own experience, the idea of their individual death can occasion a related anxiety. It is not only that we cannot imagine ourselves as nothing but also—if there is no reality apart from our own experience—our death may seem to be wholly incomprehensible. How can there be a world without *me*, since the only world I have ever known is the one that appears (directly or indirectly) to myself? If it could think, every flame and every atom in nature would have a similar thought. In overcoming our primal solipsism, we eradicate this form of anxiety. But in its more general reference, the underlying malaise may be inescapable, even in positivistic philosophers who ridicule any mention of it.

❄

In its negative aspect, ontological anxiety can make us doubt all efforts to think intelligibly about ultimate questions. Indeed, are we even sure that we know what rightly counts as "ultimate"? Being creatures who are aware of our own shortcomings, we have good reason to distrust our mental faculties. We often find ourselves guilty of self-delusion and liable to cognitive distortions of many sorts. But the uncertainties that belong to our ontological anxiety can be more pervasive. For they affect our knowledge of ourselves as conscious organisms that must define and determine their roles in the universe. We are by nature thinking beings, and if we cannot escape anxiety about the inherent structure of our thought processes, how can we hope to create purposive ideals that are congruent with reality instead of deflecting us from it?

This negative aspect may help to explain the conflict and depression that occur in many young people. I remember going through a very painful period, when I was fifteen or sixteen, during which I was troubled by reflections such as these: Not only will I die and be expunged but so too will the earth, the solar system, and possibly everything else that exists in the universe; whatever anyone achieves can have only local importance and short-lived value; in itself nothing is permanently or objectively good or bad; and therefore everything adds up to nothing and nothing really matters. And throughout these reflections, as a kind of ground bass to my misery, I sensed a residual inability to think clearly about such problems, as if they required a language I had not learned and never would. I gradually outgrew the depression that accompanied these ideas, and I am not suggesting that my depression was caused by them rather than vice versa. But they are ideas that often exist in human beings, particularly at moments of crisis, and above all in those who are beginning to suspect that there may not be a beneficent authority in the cosmos. If our ontological anxiety had only this negative pole, one might find it difficult to understand how anything but extreme pathology could ensue.

Fortunately, this type of anxiety can have a positive side. Once our hopeless questioning has reverberated in us, we may also intuit the mystery and the wonder in everything being what it is. The source of our anxiety will not have changed but our attention will now be focused on the mere fact of existence rather than the obscure possibility of non-existence. We may also experience, at least occasionally, what Wittgenstein called "astonishment that anything exists."* Instead of asking why there is something rather than nothing, we attend to the amazing—what may seem miraculous—presentation of any thing and every thing. Even if it arises out of a prior nothingness—whatever that may be—each occurrence offers itself as an ontological marvel. Though it may have been caused in every detail, the patterns of causation will themselves be experienced as gratuitous and resplendent. All reality will then appear to be what Santayana calls "free entertainment."

We feel this most keenly when goods are showered upon us beyond our expectations—serendipities or unforeseen joys, and above all the gift of a newly created life with which we can identify. When we first experience parenthood, or vicariously share it with someone else, we sense the grandeur in this augmentation of living energy. When we make something with which we have mixed our labor and into which we have poured our imagination, we feel magically renewed and revitalized. Even as hunters and fishermen, we often have mixed feelings about "the one that got away"—regret that our efforts have failed but also a sense of awe and somber gladness that this fellow participant in life can have a further chance to go on living.

Our feeling of mystery tinged with delight need not be restricted to special occasions or gratifying events. On the contrary, we may feel joyful exhilaration just in being alive, and in the immediacy with which we experience our own existence. At the end of his tormented life, Jean-Jacques Rousseau claimed to have finally discovered the sweet pleasure that comes from savoring "le sentiment de l'existence." Mysticism is a means by which some people cultivate this capacity in themselves. For most of us it is hard to reconcile the implied passivity of mysticism with the need to act dynamically in order to survive. We may nevertheless approximate the mystical attitude by enjoying, and contributing to, the development and efflorescence of life. As the baby grows, its simplest

* According to Wittgenstein, "this astonishment cannot be expressed in the form of a question and there is no answer to it. Anything we can say must, a priori, be only nonsense. Nevertheless we thrust against the limits of language."[5]

attainments strike the doting mother as uniquely wonderful. Though she is responding to her child as someone she loves in a special way, she also knows that others feel something similar when they appreciate the vivid spontaneity of life wherever it occurs. We can sense the mystery of mere existence by looking in the eyes of a domestic animal as well as in those of a human being, and in both cases we may express our enjoyment through action for the welfare of the creature to which we are attending.

To have this experience it is not essential that we love the individual whose identity we intuit. Though love is one of the means by which we acknowledge the gratuitous splendor in anything being what it is—whatever it may happen to be—we can experience a similiar wonderment even without love. We then see the object as a something that could just as easily be nothing. We immerse ourselves in the unfathomable mystery of its having the being it does have. We respond to its sheer reality, to its given but ontologically fortuitous presence in the universe. Our feeling is related to what Stendhal called an awareness of "l'imprévu" (the unforeseen) in all events. He thought that without such awareness one could not act spontaneously, or ever find the joy of living.

The state I am describing does not occur at every moment of human consciousness. For some people it is only a rare phenomenon. Even so, this feeling provides an access to meaningfulness. As long as one has such feelings, life is fraught with meaning. If we intuit the wonder in something existing and being as it is, we sense the importance of concerning ourselves with this particular entity. If we do not love the object, we may not care to preserve it. If it threatens us, we may even have to destroy it. Whatever our attitude may be, it will respond to the identity of this unique and individual being. Our life will become meaningful in relation to it.

This is not the only type of meaningfulness, and like all meaningfulness it is created by reactions that nothing can force upon us. If you are not astonished by mere existence, you cannot be coerced to have that feeling. I think of this condition as the "beginning" of meaning because it exists at such a fundamental level. Since it may not rise to consciousness in everyone, however, and since its occurrence may be infrequent in those who do have the experience, we should treat it as only one of the sources of meaning.

Among thinkers who speculate about intellectual development, wonder has often been extolled as a fertile component of human nature. In the *Metaphysics* Aristotle says it is the origin of philosophy; and Einstein remarked that a man who has no wonder about the universe is "as good as dead: his eyes are closed."[6] In Plato's *Euthyphro* Socrates shows how philosophy serves to arrest routine activities, thereby causing us to confront what is both puzzling and amazing in our actual experience. Religions have generally made a comparable attempt, and at their best they help us to celebrate the mysteries of life. When they enclose these mysteries in others of their own pseudo-scientific conception, they betray their primary mission. With innocence and purity of heart, each generation must find its own way to reinstate the initial wonderment.

The arts often exploit this experience as an aesthetic resource. Visual arts are especially suited to reveal the wonderful. A Chardin still-life presents us with apples and oranges that are very different from any real fruit we may have seen inasmuch as these are not three-dimensional and cannot be eaten. Still they express and vibrantly show forth the astounding fact that such objects, which we ordinarily take for granted, exist in a world that might just as well have had nothing like them. There they are, on the canvas as reminders of the originals that were on a plate in the artist's studio, marvels to behold just in being themselves. Music has greater difficulty in conveying this particular effect, but it readily communicates a sense of mystery. Though music can hardly represent or even get us to imagine objects existing in their individual and often mute condition, it can arouse feelings of awe, as in the opening chords of Bach's B-minor Mass, or astonishment, as in Haydn's *Creation,* or even the intuition that life is an "unanswered question," as in the tone poem by Charles Ives.

In poetry and prose we find a panoply of possible illustrations. Imagistic poems regularly encourage us, with almost simple-minded devotion, to revel in the plethora of things that appear to our senses. I choose one example from my own experience. Many years ago my wife and I attended an evening of poetry reading in a Parisian theater. It was an informal occasion and somewhat impromptu. Anyone in the audience could go up on stage and read his own poetry, or someone else's, whether published or not. One young lady, using the gestures of an actress, recited a poem that consisted of only two lines: "Il pleut,/C'est merveilleux." My wife and I both laughed. "It is raining,/That's marvellous"—this did not seem to us like much of a poem. Yet these lines have stayed with me through the years. Their diminutive structure, briefer than a haiku, the rapid rhyme signifying both immediacy and completion, expresses a feeling of wonder about mere existence. We are not told whether it is a warm and balmy rain, a cathartic cloudburst, or an exciting thunderstorm in the midst of summer. For all we know, it could be a freezing downpour. The poem merely says that rain is falling. But that is enough if one sees the common event as a marvel in itself. The force of this minimal art work would have been lessened if we had been informed about the rain's effect upon our comfort.

I find a similar instance in the second act of *Hamlet.* Telling his friend Horatio that of late he has lost all mirth, Hamlet enumerates aspects of the world that are nevertheless worthy of delight—"this goodly frame the earth," "this brave o'erhanging firmament." In the midst of his account Hamlet mentions "this most excellent canopy, the air, look you." I see him suddenly raising his eyes and acknowledging something in our ordinary experience that we normally ignore. He speaks of the *air;* he says nothing about a cooling breeze or the goodness of fresh, unpolluted oxygen. He realizes that just to live and breathe can make life worth living, if only we appreciate the wonderment in everything. In his demoralized condition, he himself is unable to do so.

Once we attain the relevant ability, we find that we can take an interest in the world apart from its utility. But, of course, wonderment does not preclude other kinds of response. Indeed, if we had no other attitude, we could not live. We are able to survive in nature only by using persons and things for our own benefit. Like it or not, we are and must be commodities for each other. If we treat another person as nothing *but* a commodity, we no longer experience him as a unique and wonderful manifestation of reality. But there is nothing to prevent us from accepting someone as he is, as a particular something that will eventually be nothing, while also profiting from his utility. Though these are very different attitudes, they may certainly coexist.

To the extent that others are commodities to us, we generally treat them as exchangeable units whose individuality has little or no significance. That is how we think about replaceable parts of a machine, for example spark plugs or transistors. One is as good as another if they all function alike. But when we cultivate our sense of mystery, the individuality in everything takes on a new importance. This importance is a value we bestow, and that is why the attitude approximates and to some extent duplicates love as I have described it in *The Nature of Love*. Life cannot be meaningless to anyone who loves. No one in love has ever asked whether anything matters. To the lover the beloved matters supremely, even if nothing else does.

But though love is related to meaningfulness, we should not assume that either is a subset of the other. Through love we make another person important to ourselves by means of our bestowal of value upon him. This may contribute to the meaningfulness of our own life, but meaning can arise in other ways as well. These other sources may also involve a kind of love—what I will call the love of life. I leave that issue for later. At the moment we do better to consider meaningfulness on its own. Similarly, we should not emphasize the role of wonderment to the exclusion of everything else. Ontological anxiety is not the only category that is basic in human experience. We are also constituted by "vital instincts," as William James calls them. These can make their own contribution to a meaningful life.

❆

The essay in which James employs this term has the title "Is Life Worth Living?" Characteristically, James begins with a jocular answer: "It depends on the liver." Does he mean the liver as the organ of digestion that so greatly controls our moods? Or is he referring to the liver as the living person who asks such questions, hoping to get an objective and all-inclusive reply but inevitably thrown back upon his own particular case?

When James examines the problem more closely, his discussion is anything but jocular. He documents the terrible sufferings human beings have undergone, the unspeakable cruelties they have inflicted on one another, and the great obstacles that attend every effort to improve their condition on earth. Far from wishing to encourage quietism or inhibit action, James thinks his horrifying account shows how meaning issues from the ever-present challenge to take up arms against a sea of troubles. If you find your existence meaningless, he says to the young man or woman in his audience, you need only recognize how abysmal life would be unless well-intentioned people like yourself accepted their responsibilities. Faced with an urgent crisis that demands moral commitment, James asserts, the ordinary person will respond. Vital instincts take over and they propel us into action that itself makes life meaningful: "A challenge of this sort, with proper designation of detail, is one that need only be made to be accepted by men whose normal instincts are not decayed."[7]

James obviously assumes that the moral imperatives with which he was reared are instinctual, or at least universal. Leaving aside this difficulty, we may also be dismayed by his implied belief that anyone who hesitates or lacks zealous dedication exemplifies the decay of "normal" instincts. We at the end of the twentieth century are likely to ask how anyone can know that such instincts exist. And if they *are* decayed, how will the Jamesian prescription be of help? The person who is floundering because his vital impulses have deteriorated will not be moved by appeals to his morality. Despite all exhortations to alleviate the sufferings of others, he will still find life meaningless. On the other hand, those who appreciate the urgency in acting as James suggests will have no need of such incentives. They will already feel that life is worth living.

One might reply that a sensitive adolescent, for instance, poised at the borderline between despair and wholesome immersion in a social cause, may benefit from the rousing appeal of Jamesian activism. This is true, and the benign character of James' preaching need not be doubted. But its actual utility is probably much less than James may have hoped.

Had he been more radical, or less eager to restore depressed humanity to health and hearty involvement, James might have raised doubts about the question with which he began. If we ask whether life is worth living, we put it in the scale with other possibilities in order to see which has greatest value. But what are those possibilities? Are we back to the absurdities of the Jewish joke about non-existence? Even someone contemplating suicide does not engage in that kind of deliberation. He thinks about killing himself because he fears that his experience will be no better in the future than it has been in the past and present. He is not evaluating life in general, only trying to decide whether he wants his share of it to continue.

In the next chapter I shall return to questions such as those that James discusses. I mentioned them here as a way of showing that an appeal to "vital instincts" requires much more analysis before it can explain how human beings create a life that is meaningful. A life of mere self-preservation, for which we may well have instincts, would be for most of us a life without meaning. We want something beyond the routine of a boring and aimless existence. We want to satisfy standards of value to which we consciously adhere. To some extent, and with tremendous variation in their level of awareness, all living things may be similar in this respect. Whether or not we believe in instincts as an underlying system of determinants, we must recognize that creatures make their own insistent demand on life: every organism acts self-righteously, as if its need to live is both obvious and inherently justifiable although dependent on other parts of nature. In its specific context, each entity asserts a claim to what is best for its own interests.

Life would seem to operate as a concatenation of discrete nodules, each manifesting its vitality from within. Something comparable may also be true of being as a whole. That was what Spinoza maintained. He held that everything always seeks to preserve, and to perpetuate, its pattern or mode of existence— "The endeavour wherewith each thing endeavours to persist in its own being is nothing more than the actual essence of the thing itself."[8] Nietzsche's notion of a universal "will to power" is also based on this conception.

I need not go that far to make my point. What strikes me as most remarkable is the fact that life expresses itself through creatures that act as if they were the center and focus of importance for all of life, as if the world "owes" them a living—as we say—and the meaning both *in* and *of* life resides in what they individually desire. I assume, moreover, that each can make this claim with as much legitimacy from its own point of view as we do from ours. I find it utterly impossible to observe another animal without seeing it as a kindred being, a bearer and representative of life just as I am, and in this respect wholly equal to myself. Everyone who enjoys the company of a cat or dog or any other pet will have had a similar experience. Though I differ in many ways from other living entities, I cannot feel that there is any ontological superiority in my being human. Life is *there* as much as *here* within me. As my own vital ends are valuable to me, I must believe the same is true for all the other myriad forms in which life occurs.

From this I derive an axiom about valuation that may help us to understand the nature of meaning. Not only do active creatures behave as if their immediate concerns are valuable, but also words like "good" and "bad," "right" and "wrong," "beautiful" and "ugly"—the terminology of value in general—must ultimately refer back to the needs, the drives, the impulses, the feelings and motives that arise from an organism's struggle to exist and promote its own particular being. From that attempt there issues a relevant type of meaning. Life has meaning for creatures that engage in the active preservation of their mode of existence.

The idea that value originates in vital demands, whether or not they are all instinctual, belongs to the naturalistic approach in Western philosophy. Thinkers as diverse as Hobbes, Hume, John Stuart Mill, Comte, James, Dewey, and Santayana have all constructed ethical systems based on this naturalistic premise. I shall not reproduce their arguments. I need only apply them to the analysis of meaning. At every moment each appearance of life makes an equal claim—though only from its own perspective—to goodness, to value, and to meaning. To see all living things this way may also increase our sense of wonder. As long as we empathize with another creature as something that is trying to secure its purchase upon life with the same self-affirmation that we ourselves feel, we cannot treat it merely as a thing, as nothing but a commodity for us to use. Even if we have to sacrifice its necessities to ours, or to the demands of a supervening morality that may require the sacrifice of our necessities as well, we will do so with humility and even reverence for the life that it contains.

I am not suggesting that this reverential attitude occurs automatically, or frequently. For though we may believe that each organism is valuable to itself, we may have little or no concern for its welfare. And regardless of our good will, we may have no compunction in subordinating its interests whenever they conflict with ours. In the order of nature there is little to suggest that animate beings often identify themselves with alien species. The lion that pounces on the antelope would seem to have no sense of unity with this other exemplification of life.

The man who slaughters an animal he wants to eat, or an enemy he wishes to destroy, will normally respond to the being of his victim much as the lion does. He acts from his own perspective. But human beings also have a deeply rooted capacity, at once conceptual and intuitive, to see the other creature as a comparable nexus of vitality, a manifestation of energy that is equivalent to what exists in them as well. When that capacity is realized, we accept the premise that our values are not uniquely justifiable, and like primitive people who worship the spirit of the animals they devour, we stand in awe before the fact that all forms of life assert themselves as an end and final embodiment of value. We are not the same as they, but we are alike in this regard.

✻

From the duality in our attitude toward life there result two modes of meaning. One of these pertains to a person's consecutive attempts to satisfy his own needs and desires. The second is a meaning that results from identification with other animate things. For our present purposes, we may put in abeyance questions about the total separability between these two types of meaning. One might plausibly argue that our ability to identify with life in others results from relevant needs and desires in ourselves. It is also possible that our conception of our self partly depends on our sense of unity with the life that others have, especially other human beings.

We shall have to return to problems of this sort. But first we should realize that each type of response contributes to meaning in life only by virtue of an intervening variable—our propensity to formulate ideals. More than any other animal, human beings are programmed to pursue distant and even unattainable goals that often serve as motives for their conduct. All organisms act in systematic and possibly agreeable ways that are needed for survival. That is why one can say that they normally have meaningful lives. The bird that builds its nest seems to care about the suitability of its building materials; the worker bees that provide food for their colony seem to act in a purposive fashion that matters greatly to them. The meaningfulness of human life is not entirely different. But unlike the bird or bee, and to a degree that is unequaled in lower primates, Homo sapiens uses his intellect and imagination to cultivate behavior that goes beyond what is needed for the preservation of either himself or others. Idealization is a notable example of this process.

To pursue ideals as human beings do is to direct one's striving toward remote achievements that are often subsumed under some imagined perfection. This goal orientation is not always prudential, for biological survival does not depend on it. Human beings do not require the works of Bach or Beethoven in order to adapt successfully to their environment. They may need the consolations of music, and in general the benefits that accrue from harmonious melody and rhythm. But lesser composers can satisfy such needs to the extent that they are merely biological. What happens throughout the ages is that human intelligence, having doubtless evolved as a device that enables our species to master its physical environment, creates infinitely varied systems of extended purposiveness. These systems become important to mankind; they acquire special value and often stimulate a further search for values. They may even cause some members of the species to believe that life is not worth living unless certain extraordinary standards are satisfied. Nevertheless, human beings could surely survive without many of the preferred ideals or valuational tropes to which they become accustomed.

Because they lie beyond our actual but meager capacities, ideals make our interests meaningful by placing them in a larger context fashioned by imagination. A feeling, an act, a momentary attitude seems meaningless to us when it occurs as an unrelated event. We need to see its ramifications within a complex of further desires and possible achievements. That is why a man who succumbs to a sexual urge for some beautiful stranger may honestly say to his wife that his infidelity meant nothing to him. Unlike Don Juan, for whom sexual conquest embodies the principal meaning in life, he may have been pursuing no erotic ideal. He experienced strong libidinal drive, perhaps, and he may have engaged in intimacies that his wife might have hoped or expected him to reserve for her alone. But in claiming that his dalliance was meaningless, he is saying that nothing really important occurred. Ideals can enrich meaning by bestowing great importance upon virtually anything we do or feel. If the wayward husband protests that his sexual fling was "just one of those things," an escapade that meant nothing at all, he treats it as a trivial event that is not related to any affective or marital ideal. If his wife is unpersuaded, it is because she sees his conduct as a threat to the network of shared ideals that define the meaning of their life together.

Similar considerations apply in other areas of our existence. People who devote themselves to a worthy but stultifying career toward which their upbringing has steered them may suddenly feel that everything they do is meaningless. This can happen to virtually anyone. In our generation it has become quite frequent, and not merely among those who have been favored in the way that Tolstoy was. A crisis of this sort occurs when men and women lose faith in the sustaining ideals with which they were raised, either because their society no longer cares about these goals or else because they themselves find them unrewarding. A man may have liked the idea of making money, for instance, but he may end up feeling that it contributes to nothing else he values. If it engages no other aspirations or attainments that matter to him, it will have lost all meaning.

For most people there is virtually no experience—not even a highly pleasurable one—that will seem meaningful unless it can be justified in terms of an ideal one has chosen. Even psychopaths have difficulty believing that whatever they happen to like is sufficient unto itself. Compulsive behavior on the part of an inveterate gambler or workaholic, or anyone else who enslaves himself to an overriding obsession, illustrates how powerful can be our need to find meaning through self-imposed ideals. The compulsiveness satisfies this need insofar as it enables an individual to pursue particular goals in a systematic and intensified manner. Betting with mystical fervor on number 7, or filling every minute with relentless toil, or diligently avoiding cracks in the sidewalk becomes supremely meaningful for such persons. They often believe that *only* these idiosyncratic ideals can give meaning to their lives.

People who are more healthy-minded, or more fortunate, idealize on a broader scale. They seek meaning through ideals that cannot be limited to isolating activities. The obsessive individual's search for meaning curtails his ability to explore. His attitude is diseased because it excludes further prospects that are available to human beings generally. When they are beneficial, ideals awaken the spirit to burgeoning possibilities for self-realization. Different ideals will be geared to different consummations, and even in the healthiest person ideals can always conflict with one another. But such constraints belong to a dynamic process that does not throttle human nature. On the contrary, it affords the maximum opportunity for creating new and more satisfying patterns of meaning.

Some thinkers, including Freud when he portrays civilization as an imposition upon biological impulses, seem to consider ideals extraneous to what is natural in us. Yet man would not be man unless he idealized, unless he constructed ideals of a deliberate and imperative character that guide his life and give it a feeling of urgency as well as direction. We might also assert that human beings would die of boredom if they somehow lost the capacity to create new standards of achievement. For an organism such as ours, idealization could thus have survival value after all. Whether or not this is true, we have evolved as a species composed of individuals who feel a constant need to pursue goals that are sometimes arbitrary and often infinitely remote.

This propensity may be uniquely human. If we can say that birds and bees act meaningfully in doing what they usually do, we may also assume that they "know" the difference between good and bad. It is good to get twigs that are solid rather than rotten, to fetch fresh rather than stale nectar. And perhaps all birds and bees have an innate sense of better or worse with respect to those elements of the environment that interest them. But we have no reason to think that *perfection* means anything to them. Or that they suffer—as human beings do—from assumed inadequacy if their efforts fail to satisfy criteria of excellence that are self-imposed and possibly a matter of individual taste.

My distinction can be illustrated by an experimental finding that at first may seem to weaken it. Ethologists have shown that in artificial conditions many species favor a pattern of behavior which is not beneficial and may even be antithetical to survival. For instance, the chicks of certain gulls are programmed to peck at a red dot on the parent's beak in order to get food. If a piece of wood is substituted for the parental beak, the chicks will peck at it provided that it too has a red dot. The bigger one makes the dot, the greater is the chick's attraction to it. In this mode of response, which can obviously be counterproductive as far as survival is concerned, we might see a parallel to the human propensity for creating ideals, establishing a gradation of values, and passionately devoting oneself to goals that make life meaningful regardless of their utility. The gulls would seem to be obsessed by the appearance of bigger and better red dots, just as some people expend their energy in the adoration of one or another type of perfectibility.

Seductive as it is, this reasoning fails in one important detail. The analogy between gull-obsessiveness and human dedication to ideals ignores the fact that in their *natural* state gulls do not show an interest in the biggest of all possible red dots. The opposite is true of men and women. Some of them, those who belong to preagricultural societies, for instance, may not care about ideals that matter to civilized people, but all human beings have a tendency to act like the manipulated gulls seeking the best red dot wherever it is to be found. What is contrived for the gulls by the experimenting scientist is natural for us. We constantly invent new ideals and yearn for unlimited possibilities. Even primitive, or unreflective humans create circumstances under which they can search for their equivalent of a perfect dot.

This does not mean that idealization is inherently directed toward perfection itself, perfection as a determinate and clearly definable entity. That concept belongs to idealist philosophies, of which Platonism is the most spectacular example. All such approaches falsify the nature of idealization. They assume that the making of ideals presupposes an ability to contemplate a purified essence which captivates us through the beauty and completeness of its form. To think in these terms is to give undue importance either to sensory acuities (above all, visual) or else to our logical faculties: the first because the philosopher interprets the pursuit of an ideal as if it were the search for a goal one observes in the mind's eye much as one directly perceives objects in a visual field; the second because the enticing perfection is generally seen as an abstract entity, like a number, as opposed to anything concrete in material experience.

We liberate ourselves from these theories of idealization by studying the search for perfection more empirically. Some people do hold aloft the image of a final, unimprovable though possibly unachievable, goal that ideally they would like to reach. The mind's eye, when it is located in the head of a particular kind of artist, does occasionally operate in this manner. For the most part, however, it does not—even for the greatest and most ambitious artists. Aesthetic creativity, like creativity in general, usually involves an endless quest toward new and ever-changing values. The artist may say that he is pursuing "the ideal," but rarely will he define it as a particular culmination that would be the absolute fulfillment of his labors if only he could attain it. Whatever he does accomplish becomes a springboard for further acts of creativity. The idea of perfection serves as a perennial incentive, but there is nothing that could be called a determinate perfection that guides his striving. Idealization functions in him, as in all of us, like a jet that propels the engine forward without any clear and distinct idea of where its trajectory must end. We are by nature internal guidance systems that maneuver ourselves through life but without any fixed or final targets.

The Platonic conception of ideals is ultimately defeatist. Despite its attempt to escape the dross of our mundane existence, despite its longing for elevated goals that reveal an infinity of aesthetic and moral goodness, despite its refusal to tolerate partial or imperfect achievements, Platonism yearns for unchanging ideals that forever float above and beyond human capabilities. They are said to motivate all our searching and yet, like the delectable fruit in the myth of Tantalus, they afford no satisfaction apart from the imaginative pleasure we get in contemplating them. The Platonist may insist that he is merely depicting the structure of reality. If frustration is inherent in all human aspiration, the fault is not of his making. He is just the messenger, he will say, bearing painful truths to mankind in the hope that we will learn how to profit from the shining essences revealed by his philosophy. Having shared his insight, will we not pursue these superior goods with greater understanding of our own limitations?

I do not dismiss this type of defense. Much of the best poetry in the Western world was written under the influence of the Platonic outlook, and without it one could hardly explain the flowering of religious mysticism in the Judaeo-Christian-Moslem tradition. All the same, this way of interpreting the nature of ideals belongs to a demoralized, and even pathological approach to human possibilities. It instills an alluring vision of goods that lie beyond each present experience, and it encourages us to take purposive action in the attempt to snare them. But then it systemically dashes every hope by asserting that nothing in the actual world, nothing in nature or the environment, is really valuable since none of it can possibly satisfy our craving for the absolute. From that remarkable assumption, this kind of theorizing concludes there must be another world or realm of being in which our losses will be restored and oneness with perfection finally consummated.

This, however, is a leap into the dark. Instead of positing an unverifiable domain in which perfectionist ideals predominate, we do better to reject all such dogmas about the nature of idealization. That faculty has an important function in human life, and we should thank the Platonists for alerting us to its pervasiveness throughout our experience. But it does not operate in the manner they envisage. As part of our life in nature, ideals provide rewards that often sustain us. We enjoy the limited degree to which we reach our goals despite their elusiveness, and we flourish through the acts of imagination and behavior that are involved in pursuing them. Though our actual achievements are not perfect, we realize that perfection is mainly a device for extrapolating beyond the status quo and that only rarely—if ever—can we hope to experience a pure example of it.

There is no inherent calamity in this aspect of the human condition, just as there is no failure in the fact that we cannot veto the laws of nature. The Platonist may be unwilling to accept the lack of perfection in the world, but to that extent he is out of touch with our reality. Those who are not will find ways to delight in the process of living for ideals that change direction as one or another proximate end is reached. Each experience of goodness serves to justify our ability to idealize. The organism is recompensed by what it has gained while also being spurred to continued action by the knowledge that ideally much more can always be imagined. A meaningful life results from this intermeshing of means and ends, purposeful efforts to satisfy ideals leading to gratifications that matter not only in themselves but also in their ability to awaken new desires and new pursuits. We do not create meaning by fluctuating between the manic-depressive extremes of Platonist metaphysics.[9]

✱

Some of the shortcomings in Plato's type of idealism were rectified by Hegel's variations on it. Hegel tries to overcome Plato's difficulties by erasing the distinction between the two realms of being. For Hegel the "other world" is simply this one seen from the point of view of its striving for greater goods. His philosophy is optimistic, not only in predicting that some day the perfect absolute will come into being, but also in claiming that every moment is a step in that direction and therefore contributes to the existence of immanent goodness. Thus ideals are always operating in nature and we need not despair even though everything we do or feel must be destroyed for the sake of some future development. If only we understood the rightness of it all, we would be grateful for our place in a world that is moving ever closer to perfection.

In effect Hegelian philosophy glorifies idealization in man while minimizing the brute materiality of the universe as a whole. To this extent it may well be guilty of what Santayana calls philosophical egotism. It is man extolling his own ability to idealize, bestowing infinite value upon this part of himself by assigning ontological hegemony to it throughout the cosmos. But even within human nature we have every reason to deny that idealization is the ultimate determinant. It is but one of many vectors interacting in our field of vital forces. Its ability to prevail is never guaranteed. And in the universe at large, there is no reason to think it has a major role to play. Ideals have great value for our species, and without them we would have difficulty explaining why many of the things that matter to us should mean as much as they do. But to extend the ontological status of ideals beyond these limits can only transmute healthy-minded self-assertion into perverse self-adulation.

Though idealist philosophies like Plato's and Hegel's may be scarcely creditable when taken at face value, or as the promulgation of literal truth, they exemplify one of our deepest attitudes. They manifest and proudly promulgate the *love* of ideals. The pervasive importance of such love should not be disregarded. When Hegel said that nothing great was ever achieved without passion, he was referring to our passionate need to serve one or another ideal. Not all men and women feel this love with the fervor and the desperate craving that belong to passion. But love occurs at various temperatures, sometimes hot and sometimes tepid. If we admit this differentiation into our thinking about the quality of love, we can readily see that the love of ideals performs a crucial function even in activities that do not lead to greatness. The idealists are therefore right in stressing, and celebrating, man's devotion to ideals. Their mistake consists in naively assuming that this type of love is necessarily preferable to all others.

To the lover, every love that is powerful seems to speak with absolute and objective authority. That is why love always runs the risk of self-delusion, as cynics have often observed (though they draw the wrong inferences). The love of ideals as felt by idealist philosophers is oblivious to the fact that some other love—for example, the love of persons—may be equally grounded in reality. Loving another person means experiencing him or her as more than just the embodiment or representation of an ideal. It means accepting this person as he is, bestowing value upon him while also appraising him in relation to one or another standard. That kind of love is different from a love of ideals, which involves dedication to them as abstractions regardless of how they may or may not pertain to actual persons.

Not only do the idealists mislead us when they ascribe ontological superiority to the love of ideals, but also they fail to admit that—for all practical purposes—their love reduces to a fascination with some ideal they personally favor. Warfare among human beings is often caused by conflict between particular ideals, each espoused with the same lofty devotion to ideals in general and the same assurance that the enemy is merely falsifying them. Passionate love can always have disastrous consequences, and the love of ideals is possibly the most dangerous. The sense of rectitude and heroic aspiration that it generates may shield our sight from the holocausts to which well-intentioned idealism can often lead.

Nevertheless, the love of ideals need not itself be impugned. I am not questioning its capacity to create a life worth living, but only its excessive glorification by an influential school of philosophers. By loving ideals we become participants in purposive behavior that expresses moral commitment and engagement in a cause beyond ourselves. Life then takes on a meaning that derives from this special kind of love. Such meaning is proof against the slings and emotional arrows that accompany the love of persons. No human being is perfect and many will not be able to reciprocate our interest. But the ideal burns brightly, like a perpetual beacon that lights our path into a terrain of ever-increasing goodness or beauty. It is Cyrano's white plume or Henry V's banner fluttering over the battlefield in Olivier's film. Though our hearts must beat responsively, and our imagination must teach us how to pursue the glittering prospect, none of this would be meaningful unless we were guided by ideals that have elicited our love—ideals of courage, truth, beauty, creativity, justice, honesty, freedom, happiness, self-fulfillment, compassion, rectitude, and even the perfection of life itself.

These ideals and others considered less noble—fame, reputation, family honor, efficiency, wealth, pleasure, comfort, social standing, eminence in a profession or sport—provide their own types of meaning. They are all created by humanity in the course of its natural and historical evolution. But as there is no prior essence that can define humanity, neither is there a preordained harmony among the ideals that different individuals or cultures must seek in their quest for meaning. The making of a unified and meaningful whole is necessary if one hopes to have a good life. But can there be a single pattern that is best for all human beings? I do not think so.

In examining this kind of problem in the following chapter, we shall have to address questions about meaning that we have thus far deferred, questions about what makes a life significant or worth living. If anything matters, how can we determine what *truly* matters? And how can these reflections help us to solve the practical problems of day-by-day existence?

4.

LIVES OF MEANING AND SIGNIFICANCE

Think of a life that has ended: a person lived, and now is dead. Imagine that someone asks whether this person had a meaningful existence. What kind of question is that? Note that we are not being asked whether the man or woman was *happy*. Despite the relation between happiness and meaning, they are not the same. We may say that happiness requires a harmonious adjustment between oneself and one's surroundings; but an individual who finds himself *out* of harmony, his experience largely consisting in a struggle against a hostile environment, might nevertheless have a meaningful life. The meaning in his life may even result from his refusal to accept the dictates of his surroundings. Given the opportunity to have a happy life if only he conforms to circumstances he considers morally repugnant, he may renounce happiness and choose uncomfortable resistance.

The hero and, to some extent, the saint are people who often feel the need to make this kind of choice. They may experience happiness, but they are prepared to sacrifice it for the sake of some goal that has greater importance for them. Though their lives are not the only ones that are meaningful, they reveal that meaning and happiness are not identical. A life without much happiness can be a meaningful one, even if—as I shall argue—a meaningful life provides its own measure of happiness.

The relationship between happiness and meaning is a dominant theme in John Stuart Mill's autobiography. Describing his life as a young man, he documents his dedication to the principles of utilitarian philosophy he had inherited from his father and Jeremy Bentham:

> I had what might truly be called an object in life; to be a reformer of the world. My conception of my own happiness was entirely identified with this object. . . . As a serious and permanent personal satisfaction to rest upon, my whole reliance was placed on this; and I was accustomed to felicitate myself on the certainty of a happy life which I enjoyed, through placing my happiness in something durable and distant, in which some progress might be always making, while it could never be exhausted by complete attainment.[1]

One could infer from this account that Mill's life at the time was both meaningful and happy. But at the age of twenty he had what he calls "a crisis in my mental development." That phrase, which he uses as the title of a chapter, is interesting in itself. For what he experienced was more than just an intellectual crisis. It was also depression or affective exhaustion. His suffering, which lasted for a period of years, taught him the difference between a meaningful and a happy life. Mill's breakdown occurred when he asked himself whether his reformist activities, his strenuous and by now habitual attempts to bring about the greatest happiness of the greatest number of human beings, would add to his own happiness if these efforts ever succeeded. He concluded that he had been deceiving himself, and that even if he did change society in ways conducive to general happiness it would not make *him* any happier.

Throughout its duration, and despite the misery it entailed,

Mill's dejected state does not seem to have undermined his pursuit of utilitarian ideals. In some respects the condition may actually have strengthened his commitment. He tells us that his pathological experience taught him that people can be happy only if they "have their minds fixed on some object other than their own happiness: on the happiness of others, on the improvement of mankind, even on some art or pursuit, followed not as a means, but as itself an ideal end."[2]

Writing many years later, Mill says that he still thinks this to be the best maxim for most people. But it does not explain the onset of his psychological crisis. All along he had been acting for the happiness of others, which he treated as his "ideal end." Yet this moral concern of his did not lead to happiness for him. It gave him something to live for, but it could not alleviate his personal distress.

Mill accurately diagnoses his problem when he says that his education had been too greatly oriented toward the acquisition of cerebral skills. Even in the midst of his crisis, he recognized that his upbringing had rendered him overly analytic and deficient in the capacity to commiserate with others. He sensed a lack of sympathetic feelings in himself. He also felt that he had attained inadequate cultivation in "passive susceptibilities" that need to be fostered as much as active and intellectual faculties. Mill associates the susceptibilities he considers passive with the imaginative pleasures that poetry, music, and the fine arts in general are able to produce. In other words, it was aesthetic responsiveness and the experience of sympathy or compassion that had been neglected in his early education. He saw now that in order to maximize the chances for happiness this area of life had to be put in balance with one's ethical and cognitive development.

Later in the autobiography, Mill shows how his enjoyment of Romantic poetry, and his love for Harriet Taylor, helped him to outgrow his previous difficulties. He does not discuss the relationship between happiness and meaning, but in other books he touches on this issue at various points. In *Utilitarianism*, for instance, it enters into his attempt to prove that there are different qualities of happiness as well as different quantities. Having asserted that no action can be morally justified if it militates against the happiness of the greatest number, Mill defends this maxim by claiming that only happiness is desirable as an end of life. At the same time, however, he insists that some kinds of happiness are "more desirable and more valuable" than others: "It is better to be a human being dissatisfied than a pig satisfied; better to be Socrates dissatisfied than a fool satisfied. And if the fool, or the pig, is of a different opinion, it is because they only know their own side of the question. The other party to the comparison knows both sides."[3]

Apart from doubts that we may have about human beings really knowing what it is like to be a pig, we may question the arguments Mill adduces to support his belief that some kinds of happiness are higher than others. He says that a "superior being" will prefer the higher kinds even though they involve a way of life that is liable to greater dissatisfaction. To explain this paradox, Mill reverts to criteria that go beyond the concept of happiness itself. He speaks of "a sense of dignity" which prevents us from exalting the happiness that would satisfy other creatures but would lessen our human capacity for intellectual and aesthetic achievement. Details about the condition Mill is advocating need not concern us. What matters here is the fact that the sense of dignity and refinement he considers paramount involves more than just happiness. Whatever the amount or type of happiness it can yield, it consists in making life meaningful by giving precedence to some of our goals at the expense of others. The "competent judges" to whom Mill appeals in determining which happiness is higher inevitably reflect their own conception of a meaningful life. People who have different ends or aspirations, and therefore create different meanings for themselves, will not agree with their judgments about the relative quality of different kinds of happiness.

We must therefore move beyond Mill's analysis. A meaningful life, whether Socrates' or a fool's, is a continuous process that includes purposive goals as well as consummations related to them. A person's behavior becomes meaningful by virtue of the ends that matter to him, whatever they may be. The world around him is then intelligible as a pattern to which his activities contribute. When these afford satisfaction, either in themselves or in their consequences, human beings are happy to some degree; and unless they have at least a modicum of happiness, it may be impossible for them to pursue most of the projects they care about. The concepts of meaning and happiness are thus interwoven. They are nevertheless distinct. We cannot explain the nature of meaningfulness merely by discovering what makes people happy.[4]

❋

How then can we determine what makes a life meaningful? The two senses of the word "meaning" that I previously mentioned—one involving cognitive clarification, the other ascribing value or purpose—can easily lead to unstable conclusions. For instance, when we survey someone's life in its totality, we may find that it lacked any outstanding purposes or controlling values that the person himself recognized and consecutively pursued. A man who has a dull and somewhat dreary existence, doing mainly what he must to keep alive, may not be aware of having any dominating purpose. Is his life therefore meaningless? He cannot avoid having values of his own; nor will he fail to act in accordance with drives that nature has generated in him. Does this prove his life is meaningful? An outsider might find a meaning in the man's life in the sense that it reveals and even typifies how people are manipulated by contemporary society, or by economic and psychological forces in the modern world, etc. But this is extraneous. It is not the kind of meaning we are trying to elucidate.

For that matter, one's own beliefs about the inner constitution of one's life may also be misleading. A man's interpretation of what his life has been does not necessarily tell us much about its meaning. He may believe that he is nothing but a trivial and disposable element within the enormous machinery of nature. Can we conclude from this opinion that his life is devoid of meaning? Certainly not. We still must find out how he actually lives despite these ideas about his meager role in the scheme of things. Regardless of how he or anyone else feels about his life, and

whether or not it includes much happiness, its meaning depends on
the purposes and values that make it what it is.

Our purposes are directed toward the fulfillment of our
desires and the acquisition of what we value. Though satisfaction
can sometimes occur gratuitously, it usually results from behavior
that is deliberately carried to completion. A meaningful life
consists of purposive activities that are satisfying either in themselves or in their culminating consummations, which are then
followed by new purposes with new consummations relevant to
them, and so forth throughout one's existence. In some areas of
life—love, for instance—the purposive and the consummatory are
so tightly conjoined that we disentangle them only with great
difficulty. In my trilogy *The Nature of Love* I attempt to do so by
analyzing appraisal and bestowal: the former as a way of searching
for benefits that people get from one another, and the latter as a
focusing of attention upon someone or something which thereby
gives that person or thing a special value. A unique, but highly
characteristic meaning results from the successful integration
between appraisal and bestowal, and from their quasi-rhythmic
cooperation, each dynamically feeding the other.

In the dogmas of most religions, it is assumed that a meaningful life must adhere to a single grand and all-encompassing purpose
that fills one's whole existence. If the plan or prior purposiveness
of some deity reveals the meaning of life, it seems plausible to think
that human beings can hope to attain meaning by accommodating
their individual purposes and values to that providential scheme.
But why limit meaningfulness in so partial a manner? Could one
not give meaning to one's life by *rejecting* the divine plan? This is
what Lucifer does. We can imagine him defending his rebellion by
arguing that though he could have attained happiness through
always saying "yea," such total and eternal acquiescence would have
prevented him from creating a meaningful life of his own. We may
even read God's willingness to tolerate Lucifer's rebellion as
divine recognition that creatures have to make their lives meaningful by themselves, regardless of any prior meaning imposed upon
them.

By discarding the usual preoccupation with a predetermined meaning of life, we also free ourselves from the Aristotelian idea that only a comprehensive "plan of life" can make a life meaningful. Aristotle thought the good life depends on rational dedication to some goal that structures one's entire being. But his view is unrealistic. At different times and at different ages a person rightly pursues different purposes. What is appropriate for a child acting out the demands of a growing consciousness that seeks knowledge and emotional expression will vary greatly from the interests he or she finds meaningful in later years. Nor should we expect all who are young or all who are old to have the same kind of goals. A life without compelling purposes, or one in which they are systematically thwarted and consummations totally denied, would not be a meaningful existence. But the fabric of meaning may vary from person to person, none of whom need have an overarching aim or super-purpose in order to make life meaningful.[5]

By insisting on this diversity, we build into our conception a pluralism that is essential for the problem of meaning as much as for other regions of philosophy. It is soothing to believe that there can be a single solution to anything, that if we train our ears properly we shall hear the legitimate voice that tells us: "This and this alone is what you must do in order to be saved." That is an enticing fantasy, but we must eschew it. The world—the actual world as opposed to a wish-fulfilling one that many people prefer—cannot sustain our yearning for such moral reassurance.

✳

I can show some of the ramifications of the pluralist approach by examining ideas about meaning that the philosopher Richard Taylor has recently offered. Taylor proposes the following as the components of a meaningful life:

> It would be a life that has a purpose—not just any sort of purpose that we happen to find satisfying, but one that is truly noble and good. And it must be one that is in fact achieved and not just endlessly pursued; and it must be lasting; and finally, it must be our *own* rather

than just something imbibed. In short, the only genuinely meaningful existence is one that is *creative*.[6]

Taylor's definition has much to recommend it. Without invoking any supernatural sanction, it describes what might be called a "high road" to meaningfulness. Mankind has always revered creativity, and people who thought themselves creative have frequently insisted that this justifies their existence. Taylor does not limit creativity to artistic production or acts of genius. He broadens the concept to include all behavior and experience that have an innovative aspect. I interpret him as acknowledging the life-sustaining character of imagination itself. And surely we may agree that human existence cannot be meaningful unless it is imaginative—which is to say, unless it surmounts the routine, repetitive, mechanical elements in life by using them for purposive activity that stimulates our thought with new perspectives, sharpens our sensations while also gratifying them, awakens our emotions to fresh possibilities of expression, and in general encourages the onward flow of consciousness to explore unknown capacities of our being. A life that is boring or without novelty is not meaningful for us.

The situation may be different in creatures that are endowed with less imaginative capacity than human beings. In one place Taylor cites the behavior of ground moles to illustrate "the meaninglessness of animal life."[7] Virtually blind, constantly burrowing underground, incessantly seeking worms or tuberous roots, forever defecating on one another, these rodents live a life that Taylor considers "pointless." It has no meaning, he says: "It is all for nothing, it just goes on and on, to no end whatever."[8] But, of course, Taylor is a human being with human interests and ideals. While using them to understand human meaningfulness, he apparently assumes that they can also explain what would be meaningful for other animals.

But why make this assumption? Though a mole does not have an imagination that is comparable to ours, either in scope or (presumably) in vividness, we have no reason to think that its mode of existence—which certainly would be meaningless for us—is meaningless for it. What Theseus in *A Midsummer Night's Dream* says of the lunatic, the lover, and the poet applies to human beings as a whole: we are "of imagination all compact." Ground moles are not. We make our lives meaningful by accepting the recurrent drudgery in them for the sake of complex and relatively cerebral goals that the imagination has made attractive to us. Other animals have other ways of living, but we need not doubt that their purposive and satisfying behavior is equally meaningful from their own point of view.

Even if Taylor allowed this modification, however, his kind of approach would still be unacceptable. When he speaks of meaningful life having "a purpose," he seems to single out one that matters uniquely in it. Perhaps he means a single network of purposes, but that also is too much to expect. Looking back at a meaningful life in its entirety, we may not be able to discover any grandiose design. The meandering trajectory may include only a broad variety of unrelated purposes. In a sense, they attain a unity in belonging to a particular life. This, however, is a trivial sense.

Furthermore, Taylor insists that meaning depends on doing what is "truly noble and good" rather than having experiences that are merely pleasant or engaging. He argues that even if an activity is meaningful to someone, it does not necessarily become meaningful *in itself.* For a man may devote his life to the mere amassing of money or, in one of Taylor's examples, the digging of a big hole. If this person believes such goals are valuable, he may think he has a meaningful existence; and Taylor agrees that his existence will be meaningful *to him.* But he denies that this kind of life will be meaningful in itself. It will not be objectively meaningful, he says, since it is not directed toward good and noble ends.

But why is this criterion essential or even relevant? Leaving aside any question of how we can *know* what is noble and good, how could such considerations apply to all meaningful lives?

One might reply that what runs counter to the truly noble or good inevitably impairs our ability to have a purposeful and rewarding life. Plato develops this argument at great length in the

Republic, and even non-Platonists have often accepted his belief that all instances of a life worth living would have to give prominence to certain preferential aspects of human nature. But having allowed this much of Plato's philosophy, the most we could infer is that some meaningful lives are not as good as others. It seems foolish to tell a man that an activity he finds engrossing is not really meaningful simply because there are other activities that are inherently better or that he would find more meaningful if only he decided to live differently. It may be true that the life we are recommending would be chosen by this particular man, and he might eventually inform us that he is now sorry to have pursued the goals that previously had meaning for him. But the fact remains that the person's life was meaningful at that time, and therefore no distinction can be made between what is meaningful to him and what is meaningful in itself.

In this respect, meaning is like pleasure. Pleasures may be delusory or short-lived or even conducive to suffering, as they may also be of a sort that we would consider disgusting or vicious, but it makes no sense to doubt that what someone experiences as a pleasure really is one. The same holds for the patterns of action or experience that constitute meaningfulness. If someone has a purposeful life that he finds satisfying, or as Taylor would say, that he "happens" to find satisfying, then that *is* a meaningful life. At least, for as long as he continues the same pursuits and finds them satisfying.

Some meaningful activities are crude or unworthy; others are harmful, either to the individual or to society; still others may be immoral. These judgments pertain to desirability, not to meaning per se. They do not enable us to distinguish between "objective" and "subjective" meaning.

Taylor also errs when he asserts that the purpose that defines a meaningful existence must lead to some lasting achievement. He gives this criterion as a contrast to the punishment of Sisyphus. Endlessly pushing his boulder up the mountain, only to see it roll back again as he reaches the top, Sisyphus is thought by Taylor (as he was by Camus) to typify the experience of meaninglessness.

Taylor argues that for the life of Sisyphus to become meaningful, he would have to achieve something—build a house or possibly a temple—instead of rolling boulders that are never put to use. This may be true, but only in the sense that a meaningful life must include consummatory experiences. Each of them is an achievement in itself. It makes no sense, however, to limit meaningfulness to any particular consummation, be it permanent or ephemeral. Constructing a lasting product is not the only way that Sisyphus can remedy his meaningless life.

Taylor claims that even if, for some obscure reason, Sisyphus enjoyed pushing rocks up a mountain while knowing they would immediately roll down again, his delighting in this process would not render it meaningful. But why not? The pleasure he derives from that activity should be recognized as an accomplishment whose value need not be disprized. It is not a "lasting" achievement, but only because no one enjoyment can last for very long. And even something that does—for example, a beautiful edifice that Sisyphus might build—is not likely to last for more than a few centuries. I shall return to the relationship between time and meaning. Here I need only remark that it is odd to think that nothing but enduring achievements are worth pursuing, or that some forms of consummation disqualify us from having a meaningful life.

Taylor's remaining criterion, possibly the most valid of them all, specifies that a meaningful existence is one that we recognize as *our own*. If a man feels bound to a routine he has not and would not freely choose—if he is a prisoner forced to do slave labor or an addict in the power of foreign substances he cannot control—he can hardly be expected to find meaning in his life of subjugation or insatiable craving. But here too we should maintain a pluralistic stance. The man whose waking hours are dominated by a compulsive need to work, as in my previous example, or to seduce beautiful women, may insist that this gives meaning to his life. Are we prepared to say that it does not? What seems to one person like meaningless enslavement may well appear to another as the creative giving of himself. Parents of devotees to some cult may feel that their children have imbibed a mind-destroying doctrine, a system of beliefs that delude and coerce in the manner of a hallucinogenic drug. But if the children claim to have found a life that is more meaningful, they may welcome their submissiveness as an expression of what they really are and really want. Even if they are mistaken, one need not doubt that any way of life can be meaningful to some extent if it has indeed been chosen as one's own.

This is not a sufficient condition for meaning; and its utility as a criterion may be more circumscribed than one might initially think. As Sartre and others have argued, human beings always retain an ultimate layer of freedom in the lives they lead. Even the prisoner and the addict can alter their existence by one means or another—through suicide, if necessary, or through an inward refusal to acquiesce in their present circumstance. In this respect, one's life is one's "own" on all occasions; and if we wish to admit some exceptions as limiting cases, they will not affect our generalization very much. But even the inalienable freedom that human beings have cannot assure them of a meaningful life. When Sisyphus—in Camus' version of the myth—casts off his meaningless state by submitting to his punishment with defiance and self-affirmation, he does more than manifest the freedom of his will. He is also asserting it in the manner of a hero. He knows what he is and what he must do. In bravely accepting his role in life, he overcomes anything the gods could have forced upon him. His meaningfulness is a function of that creative gesture, that bestowal of greatness upon himself, which he achieves by thinking and acting heroically.

❋

The pluralism I have been proposing may seem wishy-washy and overly relativistic to some people. They will feel perturbed at the suggestion that two men may have equally meaningful lives even though one of them acts for the good of others while the second cares only about his own selfish pleasures and is even immoral. Should we not distinguish between behavior that merely *seems* to be meaningful and behavior that really is? Should we not insist that being meaningful to oneself must somehow be contrasted with being objectively meaningful? If a person is devoted to the collecting of bottle tops or antique tobacco tins, we may agree that his quest for the biggest and best collection — worthy, perhaps, of inclusion in the *Guinness Book of World Records* — will provide a source of meaning in his life. But do we want to say that he therefore leads a life that is *really* meaningful? Or that it can be just as meaningful as the life of someone who struggles year after year to conquer terrible diseases, or spends decades perfecting an art, or dedicates himself to fighting injustice and ignorance? Traditional wisdom has always maintained that saintly and heroic lives are not only more desirable but also more meaningful than others.

This challenge seems formidable and must give us pause. Correctly understood, however, it involves something more than just meaningfulness. If we were to rank the hero and the bottle-top collector on a scale of greater meaning, we might sometimes give a higher rating to the latter. Beset by doubts, distractions, or a sense of personal inadequacy, the hero may have a more chaotic and less meaningful life than the one who allows nothing to deter him from his clearly demarcated goal and well-coordinated action. And yet, the traditional view is also right. For there is a kind of meaningfulness — let us call it *significance* — in which the hero's life excels.

It would appear that we now need a distinction between significance and meaningfulness in general. In ordinary language the two words are often used interchangeably. I separate them here in the hope that this bit of technical refinement will accommodate our intuition that some meaningful lives can be superior to others. Though a life may be entirely meaningful within its own dimensions, this does not guarantee that it will have much importance beyond itself.

What, then, makes a life "significant"? In his essay on that question, William James lists two principal characteristics. First, he says, there must be an ideal that is "intellectually conceived" and able to convey a sense of novelty that prevents an action from being wholly routine. Second, there must be a willingness to work in pursuit of that ideal, to labor and make concentrated efforts to realize it to the best of one's ability. According to James, what makes a life significant "is always the same eternal thing,—the marriage, namely, of some unhabitual ideal, however special, with some fidelity, courage, and endurance; with some man's or woman's pains."[9]

We may applaud these suggestions as far as they go, but they do not go far enough. The humble bottle-top collector who suddenly discovers the delights of collecting baseball cards has enriched his consciousness with a novel ideal that may possibly elicit sustained dedication. But if his interest has merely changed from bottle tops to baseball cards, if nothing else is involved in the meaning the man has now created for himself, we are not likely to believe that the new obsession makes his life any more significant than it previously was. He may find joy in moving from one ideal to the other; and given the limitations of human nature—its restlessness, its propensity to become sated with current pleasures while always hungering for greener pastures, and above all its usual inability to persevere for very long in any effort—the achievement of happiness may indeed require some such periodic alternation of ideals. They can scarcely add to the significance of our lives, however, if they are directed toward personal benefits for ourselves but not for anyone else.

This may be what James has in mind when he says that an intellectually conceived ideal provides an "uplift" and enlarges our horizons. He speaks of education as "a means of multiplying our ideals."[10] But he tells us very little about the content of these uplifting and enlarging ideals, and to me it seems crucial to emphasize that narrow or self-indulgent ideals do not make a life significant.

To some readers this remark may sound platitudinous. Particularly in the Western world, we have always been inundated with edifying proclamations designed to encourage people to sacrifice their own interests for the sake of the family, the nation, or the human race. We have seen that, despite his own experience, John

Stuart Mill was convinced that the best way to achieve well-being consists in working for the happiness of others. In human beings generally, we may wonder how often the empirical data bear out these moral prescriptions. If it is only a question of happiness or meaningful behavior, one could probably find many instances of people who lead good and wholesome lives that benefit themselves much more than others. It is true that even selfish men or women are gregarious and have feelings of affability that they may cultivate for reasons of self-interest; and like everyone else, they can expect society to make their lives miserable unless they conform to its many demands. But these are secondary considerations, since the requisite adjustments to the needs and values of other persons serve as payment for the pleasures one hopes to attain by means of them. The ideals that govern one's life may always remain in an orbit that primarily centers about gratifications for oneself.

I am not saying that everyone can find happiness and a life that is meaningful merely by acting selfishly. But I think it would be difficult to prove that no one can. That is why I introduced the further concept of significance: to show that additional conditions must be met if we are to believe that our lives amount to something. A significant life—one that is more than just happy or meaningful —requires dedication to ends that we choose *because* they exceed the goal of personal well-being. We attain and feel our significance in the world when we create, and act for, ideals that may originate in self-interest but ultimately benefit others. This mode of life comes naturally to us. It employs intelligence and imagination of a sort that is highly evolved in human beings.

The situation for most other species is quite different. As I have suggested, many animals have lives that appear to be meaningful and even happy in varying degrees. One might also say that their existence normally contributes to a biological system or ecological harmony that goes beyond their individual welfare. But this does not mean that they pursue impersonal goals for the sake of ideals that they have consciously created. Though the behavior of a queen bee may have great importance for her colony, all her activities being directed toward its survival, she is uncreative and relatively insignificant in herself. She does not formulate new types of meaning or initiate new modes of happiness. She is just the transmitter of a genetic code which she does not alter through determined efforts of her own. Any other functional queen bee would serve as well as she, and the whole life of her society is predicated upon this fundamental fact. Even if she is a mutant that introduces a novel strain within the species, she is still a conduit for material forces she cannot modify. The kind of significance that human beings recognize and care about requires more creativity than that.

As a more plausible guide to what we would consider significant, we might study the lives of dominant baboons or wolves or even sheep. Among the mammals, numerous species have a social order that reaches its apex in a leader who makes decisions for the group and possibly changes the direction of its future existence. Though he enjoys great advantages, including principal access to food and fertile females, his importance for the colony consists in behavior that is not entirely geared toward his own well-being. He must fight off invaders as well as rivals who wish to displace him. In order to retain his dominance he may have to jeopardize, and even sacrifice his own happiness to a greater extent than others in the group. As Shakespeare says, "Uneasy lies the head that wears a crown."[11]

The character in Shakespeare was talking about our own species, of course, and it is among human beings that the quest for significance becomes most interesting. Every young male baboon may want to become the dominant leader some day, and many will compete for that position throughout their lives. But so much of baboon life is regulated by laws of instinct that even those who succeed in the struggle for dominance will have little capacity to create new kinds of meaning. Moreover, there will be only one type of preeminence that makes an individual significant. For a baboon it largely consists in political power based on cunning and physical strength. Human beings can hope to obtain a significant life in many other ways as well.

Throughout the varied pursuits that make a life significant, what remains constant is the growth of meaning when this involves creation of values in the service of transpersonal ideals. The bottle-top collector may have a happy life within the special realm of meaning he has fashioned for himself, but his existence takes on greater significance when his collection attracts the attention of other collectors, when it is cited as a record-breaking achievement, when it becomes a model that strangers seek to equal or exceed. How can these peripheral reactions make one's own life more significant? By manifesting the idealist and perfectionist aspects of human nature which link a particular life with goals that matter to many others.

For one reason or another, most people do not share the interest in collecting bottle caps. We tend to place a higher value on pursuits of a different sort. But whatever the activities we may prefer, we can recognize that the significance of any life will always be a function of its ability to affect other lives. And not that alone, since our perfectionism involves a longing to create the greatest possible good or beauty to which our imagination gives us access. When asked what they would like to be remembered for, most people mention something beneficial to humanity. Beethoven's music and Mill's humanitarian philosophy are expressions of that sentiment. The greater the benefit to the greater number of lives, the greater the significance of our own. In this respect, significance does not depend on fame, power, wealth, or social standing. It depends on the value one provides—directly or indirectly—to those who can thereby make their lives happier or more meaning-ful or even more significant.

I realize that words like "benefit" or "value" are very vague. Partly this results from the fact that what is beneficial for one person may be harmful to another. Moreover, different people or societies create different ideals and therefore different notions of well-being. Whether we opt for a relativism which considers such disparity unavoidable or seek objective standards that reveal what is truly beneficial, a particular life can have significance only insofar as it augments the meaning and happiness of life as a whole, regardless of any effect upon one's own desires.

＊

Schopenhauer claimed that someone's life is real and important only as an enlightened manifestation of the unitary life-force which is Being itself. That was why he considered the sense of individuality to be an illusion as well as the cause of human suffering. Our ordinary experience is futile, Schopenhauer thought, because this fundamental fallacy encourages us to pursue selfish goals predicated upon the belief that we are each a separate substance. He extolled the faculty of compassion because he thought that it alone enables us to perceive our oneness with all other living creatures, recognizing them as fellow victims within the single reality of life. Though we are insignificant as mere units of vitality that foolishly think ourselves unique and independent, we become significant once we identify with, and act to benefit, every other manifestation of life.

This part of Schopenhauer's philosophy is tempered by his unrelenting pessimism, which insists that human efforts cannot do much to alter the universal misery in animate existence. But if that is true, one cannot believe that even a significant life adds up to very much. Though he builds his moral philosophy on an identification with all living things, Schopenhauer would seem to denigrate life from every point of view. In human beings the general degradation appears as either an illusory sense of individuality or else as compassionate feeling that can have virtually no effect upon the world one wants to change. We might very well infer that no form of life can ever be really significant.

We escape this baleful conclusion not only by avoiding metaphysical assumptions such as Schopenhauer's but also by advancing a different view of nature. Humans—and possibly some other animals as well—have a double being: we are conscious of ourselves both as individuals and as manifestations of life. Neither self-conception is illusory. As individuals, we act to preserve our own existence as well as the existence of anything that can help us survive. When we succeed in this endeavor and enjoy the process, the reward is happiness; the penalty for failure is depression, disease, and premature decay. As persons who are happy, or hope for happiness, each of us wants to go on forever and we are saddened by the realization that this will not happen and may even be impossible. We may want to prolong our lives indefinitely, but we suspect that everything in nature disintegrates and finally disappears. Though we may cling to theories about life in another world after death, we also—and often simultaneously—fear that they are all implausible. To some extent, everyone who thinks about the matter feels that his existence must be finite.

If we had nothing else in consciousness, our fixation on our approaching doom would make life an unalloyed horror—as it often is for inmates in a concentration camp or prisoners on death row. Instead, we mitigate the sentiment of dread by fulfilling our nature not merely as persons who live or die within our separate being but also as expressions and embodiments of a life that includes more than just its particular manifestation in ourselves.

In cultivating this further attitude, we move beyond our individuality and diminish our concern about its finitude. We expand our own selves by creating additional selves that issue from us: children who can live on when we are gone. We make material objects that will enter into the experience of others whether or not we are still alive. We create institutions and engage in pursuits, as in science or technology or the humanities, whose accomplishments endure long after we have died. Much of human imagination is activated by goals that have only a tenuous or indirect relation to our own personal existence. Fame may be the spur, as Milton said, but also part of our being—in varying degrees, no doubt— identifies with life as it occurs in other creatures. Though our efforts are often thwarted, we try to put ourselves in their position, to see the world from their perspective, to imagine what life in them is like. All poetry and fiction arise from this inclination. We also learn about ourselves by analogy to others, and through their immediate or eventual conception of us. Since we depend extensively on other people, our sympathetic awareness of them readily turns into concern about their welfare.

When this element in our nature combines with our faculty of idealization, there results the kind of behavior that seeks to preserve and to improve life beyond ourselves. This mode of response, reinforced by explicit achievements that enable us to believe the enterprise is succeeding, makes our life significant. For life is then propelling itself into new approaches to perfectibility, transcending the littleness of any individual. In view of what we are, where else could we hope to find significance in our lives?

Thus significance is more than just the attaining of meaning or happiness in one's own life. It derives from an imaginative struggle for meaning and happiness in other lives, even when the effect upon ourselves is not to our advantage. Under ideal conditions, we would increase our happiness and find ever greater meaning through acts that augment the quality of life wherever it occurs. But that is an impossible dream: the world is not ideal. Life as it appears in the AIDS virus is inimical to life in human beings. We cannot hope to preserve and perfect both simultaneously. But then, one might ask, what does it mean to preserve and perfect life in general?

The argument seems to have reached an impasse. One could easily cut the knot by saying that concern about life as such is just an illusion, a cunning device of self-love. That, however, goes against all observation. The mother who carries a child within her will often have no perception of it as a benefit to herself. On the contrary, she may feel that she is merely the source and fertile receptacle out of which this new existence will come forth. If she wants the child, she wants it for reasons that neither she nor anyone else may fully understand. She has an impulse to create life, an instinct to propagate a living entity that continues her being but also exists apart from her own individuality. In the mythology of many peoples, women are regularly represented as the bearers of life, the vehicles that it has chosen in its unrelenting self-assertion. Such myths are primitive, but they are primitive in us all. And they become persuasive when we recognize that, in their own way, men also convey life. They bear not only the seeds from which it grows, but also the social constructs—created by members of both sexes—in which it shows itself as surely as in its material embodiments.

If the ideal of protecting and perfecting life had no influence on human behavior, we could hardly understand the great preoccupation that many people have about the world as it will be after they are dead. One might say that wills and testaments, endowments, plans for some remote future are simply imaginative devices by which we try to perpetuate our own values, and thus pretend that we are prolonging our existence beyond the grave. Though we know we may not live to see our great grandchildren, we bestow a fictive longevity upon ourselves by participating vicariously in the world that they will have. This explanation is partly correct. But our interest in the future also reveals a concern about the preservation and improvement of life, at least as it occurs in manifestations that we care about. The ideal of leaving the world a better place than when we entered it has been a motive force in the lives of many people. It may often be reduced to little more than a desire to improve the lot of one's own children (or of one's gene pool, as the sociobiologists would say) but this alone does not account for the efforts that are often made on behalf of other animals and unrelated human beings.

In these final years of the twentieth century, we have a striking example of the attitude I am trying to describe in mankind's fascination with space travel. No one has suggested that life on earth will disappear or become untenable for centuries to come. Neither can anyone believe that the material and technological pay-off in the proximate future will balance the huge expenditures that extra-terrestrial exploration involves. What fires our imagination and justifies the heroic deeds of our astronauts is the feeling that life as we know it, which may be the only life there is in the universe, must find some way of continuing even after the extinction of our planet. Though *we* cannot go on, we feel that life must do so. Our individual death will have lost some of its bitterness if in living as we did we contributed to the furtherance of life beyond ourselves.

I am not suggesting that the ideal of preserving and perfecting life takes precedence over all others as a matter of objective necessity. We need not agree with those metaphysical idealists who say that everything is motivated by a longing for greater and better life throughout the universe. No ideal is ontologically supreme. Like all ideals, this one must struggle as a partial vector within the field of forces that nature is forever germinating. It has no inherent priority, and its relative importance is always subject to circumstances that are constantly in flux.

If this is what we believe, however, why *should* anyone pay much attention to what does or does not improve other lives—to say nothing of life as a whole? We have been studying the nature of ideals, above all the devotion to life itself, as a way of explaining what can make our existence not only meaningful but also significant. But if significance arises from pursuing an ideal that is itself variable and haphazard, or at least lacking in objective authority as far as the cosmos is concerned, why would anyone risk an iota of well-being in order to have a significant life? Why think that this aspect of our nature really matters? Indeed, why should we think that anything does?

❄

In Camus' novel *The Stranger* a depressed and somewhat psychopathic young man commits a senseless murder. Dazzled by the sun and acting on an impulse he himself cannot understand, he kills someone on the beach who happens to annoy him. The murderer is arrested and condemned to death. When a priest entreats him to confess, he reacts violently and shouts: "Nothing matters."

Analyzing the character's use of language, R. M. Hare argues that it should not be taken as referring to any objective state of affairs. Hare suggests that when we say something does or does not matter we are merely expressing our own concern about it, or else the concern some other person has (in which case we would say that it does or does not matter "to him"). Hare means that the word "matter" in this context cannot apply directly to any thing or condition in the world but only to someone's feelings about it. Asserting that nothing matters is just the character's way of informing us that nothing has importance for him; and therefore his statement should not be treated as a comment upon the universe at large. According to Hare, it only reveals the man's dejected and defeated state of mind on this particular occasion. The language would not be appropriate in a different situation or for most other people, since they are obviously concerned about many things—the quality of their breakfast, their continued good health, etc.[12]

Hare's analysis does an injustice to Camus and to his protagonist, each of whom may surely be interpreted as making claims about the universe. Both are insisting that, regardless of what matters to them or to other human beings, nothing is *really* important. In other words, no interests and concerns that define our values can be justified or even corroborated by independent facts. Various things matter to one or another person, but nothing matters in any further context and therefore nothing truly matters.

If this is what Camus does intend, one might immediately offer two responses diametrically opposite to each other. For many people, it will suffice to reply that if something matters to someone it really does matter and that's that. What other criterion is needed? What other validation would count for very much? Isn't Camus assuming, naively but falsely, that individual mattering is somehow insufficient, as if we might possibly hope to discover a higher standard or authority which he himself does not believe in? The other kind of answer is typified by the *reductio ad absurdum* I mentioned earlier: If nothing really matters, then neither does it matter that nothing matters.

Both responses are entirely legitimate, and each helps to protect us from the demoralization that often accompanies the belief that nothing matters. The first does so by emphasizing that however trivial our interests may be in a different frame of reference—in relation, let us say, to superior beings who inhabit another galaxy—there can be no justification for denying that they really matter to *us*. The second answer serves to quiet the uneasiness that we may feel in questioning the actual importance of what we care about. For if nothing does matter, we need not allow this fact, unimportant like all others, to affect our behavior or emotions very much.

Though these replies can be reassuring, they will not satisfy everyone. Hidden as it may be, a desire lurks in human beings to get beyond their glassy essence and smug contentment with what is merely of value to themselves. Moreover, a person who is upset by the idea that nothing matters apart from someone's interest may be further troubled by the suggestion that this advance in his ability to think has no greater importance than anything else. In concluding that nothing matters, he had hoped to reach a level of insight that would afford him a secure understanding of himself in relation to the world. If this cognitive achievement also does not matter, he might well feel even more demoralized than before.

In trying to resolve this problem, we should begin by recognizing how comforting it can be to think that nothing matters. Dr. Johnson, the eighteenth-century moralist, advised those who suffer from the belief that they have committed a social faux pas to imagine how miniscule the event will seem twelve months later. Having made a fool of yourself in public, you may feel anguish that certainly matters to you at present. But in time it will diminish and probably disappear. Even if you do not forget the experience, others will: it will be smothered by all the subsequent happenings that eventually push it into oblivion. Something similar can be said about most of our failures. If we see them from the vantage of some future epoch or remote corner of the universe, we are likely to free ourselves from acute remorse and "agenbite of inwit," as James Joyce calls it. We are tranquillized by the idea that "this too will pass."

By extension, this kind of remedy may be applied to everything that matters to human beings. Idealist philosophies have often encouraged us to assume a cosmic perspective on all things temporal and merely natural. We are told to envisage them from God's point of view or in terms of absolute spirit. The concept of "the eternal" was constructed with that in mind. Seeing all things under the aspect of eternity implied a recognition that, despite its apparent or current importance to oneself, nothing could possibly matter in comparison to the ideal reality which is the foundation of being. If we truly subscribed to this article of faith, would we not be bolstered by the assurance that our daily and inescapable struggle for existence, for happiness, for rectitude, and even for the preservation of those we love does not really matter? At the very least, we would no longer be tormented by our knowledge that sooner or later our works and efforts will all be buried in the sands of time.

This anodyne in idealist philosophy is nevertheless hurtful. It lessens the painfulness of seeking endlessly for the goods of this world, but only by denying their inherent goodness. Moreover, it increases our sense of failure, instead of counteracting it. Though our merely natural shortcomings will not matter to us as they might have previously, neither will anything else that belongs to our condition. Striving for transcendental goals that can never be satisfied by our existence in nature, we shall be laden with a feeling of inadequacy more total and more devastating than before. The darker side of all religions—the part that issues into asceticism or assurance of original and ineradicable sin—shows how frightening the consequences of idealism can be.

As opposed to these gross distortions of the human spirit, how much saner and more benign is the deflationary idea that really nothing matters! Like a mother who tells her child that he can do no wrong, the nihilist approach may bring its own kind of blessed peace. Without terrifying us by a contrast between the meager, ephemeral lives that we lead and the infinitely greater importance of absolute ideals and underlying realities, the belief that nothing matters can make us tolerant of each other. By ridding us of pomposity and autocratic self-righteousness, it may even help us to become more compassionate. What it cannot do is to provide a motivation for living, an energy to keep on going despite all impediments, an élan or vital impetus that declares the value and imperative necessity in doing one thing rather than another.

To discover these aspects of a viable solution, we need a different approach. We have considered, and found wanting, the notion that some thing or principle beyond the empirical world might reveal what really matters. In searching for an alternative, we should ask why it is that human beings raise these questions in the first place. Other animals, with their inferior intellects, are not prone to such dilemmas. Unless they are imprisoned by our species or poisoned by noxious elements in the environment, for which humans are also usually responsible, they live meaningful lives and that is what matters to them. When someone asks whether anything *really* matters, the intellect has created a gulf between that individual and his origins in nature. The intellect does not operate in isolation, of course. It is basically a tool that vital interests use for purposes of survival and mastery. If those interests have been crushed or weakened, as happens in states of despair and pathological disorientation, the intellect readily becomes subservient to these new conditions and—like the sorcerer's apprentice—it multiplies the difficulties of life without being able to control them.

The person who convinces himself that nothing matters has lost contact either with the instincts that would normally direct him toward his own well-being or else with those that bind him to other creatures. To act as if nothing matters is to thwart the innate program of life itself. It is in their nature for all living things to find something (and usually a great deal) that matters to them. Human beings are able to minimize this aspect of themselves as they may also commit suicide or even destroy all life on the planet. This does not mean that ultimately nothing matters, but only that we are free—if we so choose—to bring about an end of mattering.

Once we ask whether anything matters we thus entangle ourselves in logical problems about the concept of life. The question is asked on the assumption that living creatures exist and that something might or might not matter to them. But part of what we mean by life or being alive includes the idea that various things do matter to some organism. If we assert, on a particular occasion, that what matters to one or another person does not *really* matter, we mean that greater importance is, or should be, ascribed to something else. Even when there is no way of adjudicating among these different claims, what we call life requires us to make them.

It might seem that I am merely reminding the skeptic that many things matter to individuals and therefore that one cannot say that nothing does. But I wish to go beyond that. For we are constantly changing our ideas about what matters; and it is always proper to ask whether something in particular really matters. If someone replies "It does to *me*," that ends the problem. It is not that we believe the other person has an infallible authority or will not renounce his statement at some later date. It is just that we see in him, and in his remark, a demonstration of what it is to be alive. By its very nature, all life manifests active choice and selectivity. In creatures like ourselves this means having a preference for one or another possibility and therefore wanting it to exist. That is what makes something matter.

But we often say that one thing matters more than another, don't we? Yes. And we also know that what matters to one person does not always matter to anyone else. How then can we tell what *truly* matters? And if someone denies that anything does, is he not asserting that no sanction exists for choosing one particular system of values rather than another? How have we strengthened the argument by saying the nature of life requires that something matters to whatever lives? This might be of interest if there were a single goal or principle that matters most to everything, but otherwise how does our probing help us determine that anything really matters?

The discussion can be useful by directing attention to what might be called the "ontological biogrammar" of each living thing. It is not by chance that something matters in the universe, for this is part of the definition of life once it comes into existence. Our conception also serves to elucidate the double being of man to which I previously referred. Insofar as man experiences himself as a separate individual, what matters to him is anything that brings about his own happiness and sustains the meaningful life he has chosen. Insofar as he is one among other manifestations of life, however, and perceives himself as such, he becomes aware that what matters to other creatures matters equally and really does matter. This growth of consciousness is not automatic. It is gratuitous, like all spiritual development: it harkens freely to a pervasive but ignorable fact about life and is not motivated by an exclusive desire to promote our own material interests. In its own way, it enlarges our capacity for self-fulfillment. It expands our pattern of meaningfulness, giving increased value to what matters for others as well as what matters for ourselves. In beings such as we, that is what really matters.[13]

❅

I propose this way of thinking in order to use what is best in Schopenhauer's ideas about identification with other embodiments of life while avoiding his vitalistic dogmas. Compassion does not require an intuition of underlying unity, as Schopenhauer thought, but only sympathetic recognition that life in others—as in ourselves—includes a concern about something that matters. What matters to the other may not matter to us, but in feeling compassion we show that we care about this different exemplification of the life we have in common. Out of this there arises (though not ineluctably) an interest in preserving, extending, and improving life in general. And that, I have suggested, is what enables human beings to have lives that are truly significant, not merely meaningful or conducive to happiness.

But what exactly does it mean to preserve, extend, and improve life? Each species acts as if its own survival fulfills the content of these demands. And within our species, there is endless diversity among the notions of perfectibility that guide behavior. Even Nazi ideology, which almost everyone abhors nowadays, claimed that it sought to purify the human race by eliminating soft and sentimental attitudes that run counter to the deepest stirrings of nature. Though different in many respects, this dreadful delusion is on a par with Spinoza's idea that the excellence of human reason justifies our subjugating less rational creatures; and both may derive from the biblical belief that man is uniquely the child of God and therefore entitled to dominion over all other forms of life. These doctrines would seem to satisfy my criteria for significance as fully as Albert Schweitzer's "reverence for life." Is this a consequence we are willing to accept?

To some extent, we must. The Nazi philosophy was able to beguile as much of humanity as it did precisely because it promised a significant life to those who were willing to sacrifice everything to it. Evil as it was behind its idealistic veneer, it satisfied the heroic imagination of many people who saw no other possibility of achieving a meaningful life. It pacified their doubts about whether life is worth living by providing a cause for which they were even willing to die. Having subdued this particular nightmare of the twentieth century—though new ones keep occurring—we must try to invent healthier and more desirable ways of making life significant.

CONCLUSION

The Love of Life

In Ingmar Bergman's film *The Seventh Seal* Death agrees to play a game of chess with a knight who is returning from the wars. The knight can go on living as long as the match continues. In one scene Death, posing as a father confessor, tricks him into disclosing his strategy on the chessboard. The knight's first reaction is a surge of indignation at this treachery. But suddenly he feels his own importance as one who has survived thus far and is playing the game, which is life itself. "This is my hand," he says, "I can move it, feel the blood pulsing through it. The sun is still high in the sky, and I, Antonius Block, am playing chess with Death!" In the background we hear celestial voices intoning the goodness in this moment of self-realization.

The knight has experienced what Joseph Campbell calls "the rapture of being alive." It is an exhilaration that everyone desires. Nevertheless, it alone cannot tell us how to cope with our reality as human beings. Problems of life and death cannot be resolved by any feeling, however rapturous. The knight intuits that he must go beyond his momentary exaltation by enacting "one meaningful deed" that will complete his mission on earth. In doing so, he preserves life and defeats death, though he himself dies in the process.

But is a single deed capable of providing an adequate solution? If so, what kind of deed must it be? If not, how should we characterize the multiple deeds that may be needed? My argument has been gradual throughout this book, and one can wonder about its practical implications as well as its direction. The reader may possibly have turned to this concluding chapter in the hope of finding an inspirational bottom line. I will try to satisfy this demand but I fear that the cat I let out of the bag may only be a scrawny kitten.

I have sought to lead attention away from questions about the meaning of life, as if there were only one and as if it were a prior reality that can be discovered. I have emphasized that human beings *give* meaning to their existence, and that they do so by creative and increasingly imaginative acts that reveal what matters to them as living entities in nature. I distinguished between happiness and meaningfulness as a way of suggesting that a life filled with meaning may not always be an especially happy one. Though a meaningful life provides many gratifications, and though happiness requires a certain degree of meaningfulness, the two conditions are not necessarily proportionate to one another. I argued that philosophers who use happiness as the sole or supreme criterion of the good life are neglecting a quest for meaning that may be more important in human nature.[1] And I also recognized that we characteristically seek experiences that are more than just meaningful for us as separate individuals. I claimed that a truly significant life would be an innovative one that is devoted to the preservation and perfecting of life itself. This idea is, however, vague and unsettling. How can we make sense of it?

From the outset, I have resisted the seductive assurances of optimists who tell us that in life all is for the best and that beyond (or even within) our vale of tears an ultimate, though possibly unknowable reality sustains and justifies man's finest aspirations. There is something in the phenomenology of experience that makes me distrust such theories about our predicament. Our mere existence in time, as creatures whose immersion in past and future prevents us from adequately *realizing* the present, convinces me that the optimists are deluding themselves.

What I am referring to appears in the final act of Thornton Wilder's play *Our Town*. Having died in childbirth and taken her place in the local cemetery, Emily returns to the world as a spectator of her own previous existence. On the advice of others among the dead, she has chosen to observe a happy but relatively uneventful day in her life. It is her twelfth birthday, and she watches the day as it unfolded for herself and for her family. She is astonished to see how young and beautiful everyone looks, as we often feel when we come across old photographs. But what brings tears to her eyes, and to ours, is her sudden awareness that we never really savor or consummate our being in time. It is as if time, as we live it, is something we cannot fully experience. It is always escaping us. We always seem to be out of phase, unable to synchronize our feelings and our needs with time's uncontrollable movement. "I can't go on," Emily says, ready now to accept her burial in the earth: "It goes so fast. We don't have time to look at one another. [She breaks down sobbing.] I didn't realize. So all that was going on and we never noticed. Take me back—up the hill—to my grave." Before leaving, she asks the Stage Manager: "Do any human beings ever realize life while they live it?—every, every minute?" No, he replies, but then adds: "The saints and poets, maybe—they do some."[2]

The Stage Manager's answer is ambiguous. Does he mean that some saints and poets may possibly realize life at every minute? Or else that they do so but only on some occasions and to some degree? In either event, one might say that the playwright himself helps us toward the realizing of life merely by portraying our usual inability to do so. This is part of the aesthetic value in art, and I am not questioning its life-enhancing goodness. But like Emily and the Stage Manager, I feel the unredeemable sadness out of which artistic effort arises.

In the history of philosophy a long line of thinkers—from Plato to Alfred North Whitehead, Paul Tillich, and others in our century—have developed concepts of "eternal objects" that are different from the content of temporal experience.[3] We get "out" of time, they say, when we liberate ourselves from the headlong plunge of past-present-future. By stepping back from the temporal, by contemplating its given qualities without considering what precedes or follows them, what causes or results from them, we realize that which is timeless and therefore eternal in every moment. But beautiful as this vision may be, it is, I believe, simply untrue to reality. The qualities or formal properties to which these thinkers refer are just abstractions—like mathematical truths or logical tautologies. They do not acquaint us with the full concreteness of experience, with life as it is actually lived not only from moment to moment but also in every single moment. Eternal objects are snapshots of reality, and therefore static. Life is not.

This does not mean that we must eschew the artificial definition of the eternal that philosophers have offered us. We may sometimes meet their criteria for "living in eternity," if we so desire and have received an adequate training. But while we are enjoying this particular experience, we still belong to life as it flows on; we remain participants in the temporality from which we tried to emancipate ourselves. And if that flux is tragic because of its basic unrealizability, it is doubly so when we allow our intellect to fabricate glamorous language that merely disguises the inescapable. Nor can we learn to love life by seeking means of denying or ignoring its dismaying reality.

What follows from all this? Shall we spend our days gnashing our teeth and agreeing with the character in Euripides who claims that "all of human life is filled with anguish,/Nor is there remission from its sorrow"?[4] Many people have thought that the belief in immortality offers an avenue of joyful expectation. If our present condition is melancholy, they say, can we not hope for goodness in some life after death that continues for a non-finite duration? But why think that time will be any different then? If we cannot realize temporal existence in this world, why think that we would be able to do so in one that goes on for very much longer? In the *Tractatus* Wittgenstein remarks: "This assumption [immortality] completely fails to accomplish the purpose for which it has always been intended. Or is some riddle solved by my surviving forever? Is not this eternal life itself as much of a riddle as our present life?"[5]

Elsewhere Wittgenstein states that "a man lives eternally if he lives in the present."[6] Possibly he means a man who takes each moment as it comes and neither dwells upon the past nor worries about the future. That kind of life may be blissful but it would not free us from the limitations of temporality. Whatever our life in the present may be, and however long it might last, we are still bound by the constraints of our existence in time.

The Hindu concept of karma may seem preferable to Western ideas about an immortality that cures the malady of man's temporal being. In the twentieth century, at least, we are likely to share the sentiments of the character in John Mortimer's play *Voyage Round My Father* who says he cannot imagine anything worse than "living for an infinity in some great transcendental hotel with nothing to do in the evening." If our immortality follows the pattern of karma, however, there is always something to do. Each life a person undergoes has a mission: to purify the eternal soul that recurrently dips into materiality, like a pebble skipping across the waters of time. This alone would serve as a meaning to life in general. But karma cannot explain why the purification of a soul should matter, or even its existence. And unless the totality of successive incarnations is worthwhile in itself, one cannot infer that a single segment within the trajectory—for instance, the life we are now living—has any value.

We have thus returned to our earlier questions: Is life worthwhile? Is life worth living? Though closely related, these are in fact two different questions. The former pertains to the value of life in its entirety. It is the kind of question that the Judaeo-Christian God, who is presumably beyond life though also alive in some sense, might have asked himself when he first contemplated creating a universe. Is it better, he may have wondered, to have laws of nature that produce animate as well as inanimate beings? Since life abounds on our planet, we may think that this deity saw some value in having both living and non-living substance. But whether or not we believe in any such creator, we must give some thought to the original question: Is a cosmos that has life in it more valuable than one that does not? In other words, is life itself worthwhile?

This is quite different from inquiring whether life is worth living. For that is what an individual may ask about his own participation in life, or the participation of others. Even if life is worthwhile in itself, its occurrence in us may not be such as to warrant the struggle to stay alive as long as possible.

The first question is very puzzling. It is one of the facts about the universe that life exists in it. We observe life in other creatures and we experience it in ourselves. Can we ever attain a vantage point from which to decide whether the universe is better or worse because it does include life? It is even problematic whether we can say it is better for *us* that there should be life. For what we mean by "us" already presupposes that we are alive. Possibly the question lingers as a vestige of beliefs in another type of being, that spirit-world in which disembodied souls survive their natural demise. But that is not our world, and whatever may define their being can represent life only in an obliquely symbolic manner.

Even so, one might say that there is nothing illogical in asserting that animate nature—including our own—either does or does not have value. One could then go on to claim that the universe is better because it has life in it, or else that it would be better without life. But using language this way, how could we explain the meaning of the valuational terms? Words like "worse" or "better" refer to what matters to living creatures. In a world without them, how would anything be more or less worthwhile, or valuable in any sense? Possibly one might say that life is so painful or pernicious that even from the point of view of its own values it is not worthwhile. In effect, this reduces the first question to the second one: it implies that, in all animate beings alike, life is not worth living.

That suggestion appears in the joke I cited in an earlier chapter about the two old friends who discuss the lives they have had. Though he has a good life, one of them asserts that he would prefer not to have been born at all. In a similar vein, Byron tells us that "whatever thou hast been,/'Tis something better not to be"; and a Chorus in Sophocles expresses the idea that "never to be born is far best."[7] A contrary view is held by those who believe that life is *always* worth living, regardless of how wretched or absurd it may be. This assertion has been made by Camus, but it was already present in Homer's *Odyssey*. Though he is now a king among the shades, Achilles insists that any condition of life—however lowly or miserable—is preferable to being dead. An extension of this idea occurs in a seminal article by Thomas Nagel. Attempting to prove that death must always be an evil, Nagel claims that life is inherently worth living. Over and above the elements in experience that make life better or worse, he argues, there remains something that has positive value. This is "experience itself, rather than . . . any of its contents." According to Nagel, that additional factor makes life "worth living even when the bad elements of experience are plentiful and the good ones too meager to outweigh the bad ones on their own."[8]

But can the experience of life be evaluated in isolation from all its contents? Apart from its good and bad elements, there is no human experience. There is no substratum of experience to which good or bad elements may be added but which remains "emphatically positive," as Nagel says, whether or not they are added. Experience is always good or bad in some respect, satisfying or unsatisfying, rewarding or unrewarding. It is always hedonically and affectively charged. As a result there cannot be a residue that provides an underlying value capable of outweighing bad elements. If we eliminate all positive and negative contents, we eliminate experience itself and reduce human life to the level of a plant or vegetable.

Is there an inherent good in being a vegetable? If they could speak, some vegetables would surely say there is. But the life of a vegetable must also consist of good and bad elements, healthy and diseased components. By extending the argument to their condition, we have done nothing to demonstrate that life either is or is not worth living.[9]

As a possible solution, I suggest that life is worth living when its good elements outweigh the bad but that life is not worth living when the bad greatly predominate and there is hardly any goodness left. In making such judgments, one must always factor in predictions about the future and hopes about events whose outcome is still unknown. The meaning of "good" and "bad" will have to be determined by the speaker's standards of value, and these can obviously differ from person to person. But what matters most is the fact that no life carries with it a prior assurance of its own permanent worth.

We may also say that those who feel that life is worth living are manifesting the goodness in their own experience, and their buoyant confidence that in the future some semblance of this goodness will continue. This projection may be accurate to some extent, and in any event I have no desire to undermine whatever sustenance such belief may bring. It can be a life-preserver and therefore self-fulfilling as a prediction. It is part of how we make life worth living, assuming a virtue in experience—to reformulate what Hamlet says to Gertrude—even if it has none independently. This feat of the imagination is often benign and beneficial. It need only be understood for what it is.

My approach has implications for practical moral issues. If life is not worth living when the bad elements vastly outweigh the good, we have less reason to prolong the existence of those who are terminally ill and incapable of experiencing more than pain or unbearable misery. We may have other grounds for opposing euthanasia or suicide, and each patient must be encouraged to consider the possibility that his suffering may someday be alleviated. We shall also have to gauge the consequences to others if this individual's life is either extended or curtailed, to say nothing of the danger in making such decisions at all. But the premise about life being *inherently and necessarily* worth living, which is sometimes assumed in these deliberations, will no longer apply.

❅

Having come this far, however, we may still wonder where our exploration has led us. In order to determine what truly matters and contributes to a significant existence, I suggested that the preserving and perfecting of life—unclarified as this conception may still be—affords an outstanding kind of meaning. But if I say that life is not always worth living, am I not negating the importance of that vital principle in the service of which we were supposed to attain our own significance? Must I now revert to the comfortable relativism of those who claim that nothing matters objectively and that what does matter varies in accordance with the particular meanings each person individually creates?

This solution is unpalatable because it neglects the character of our striving for perfection. Human beings seek for unlimited goodness not only in projects that benefit them as separate individuals, but also in relation to life beyond themselves. The baseball player who pitches a no-hitter will have accomplished something meaningful, but it is a significant achievement only to the extent that his skill warrants the approbation of people who know the game and delight in seeing it played perfectly. The pitcher does not merely wish to trounce his opponents. He wants to do so in the context of an activity, the sport of baseball, that enriches life for all its fans and players. The more that an art form or communal enterprise fulfills such ideals, the more significant it becomes. Its significance consists in the wealth of meaning that it makes available to human beings and thus, in that degree, to life itself. By adding to this fund of meaningfulness, individuals attain their own significance.

What is significant in life, and what makes us feel our own lives are significant, involves participation in creative acts that lead to greater meaning in the cosmos. This is the message, albeit crammed with distressful metaphysics, that Hegel and the nineteenth-century Romantics conveyed to us in the modern world. But also, I suggest, these creative acts are morally justified only in relation to utilitarian principles about the greatest happiness of the greatest number of human beings and—wherever possible—all other forms of life. Though their benevolence was normally limited to mere humanity, the utilitarians who attacked Hegel from the bastion of their empiricism were more reliable moralists than he.

My statement skirts many difficult problems in ethical theory. But that is not the subject of the present book, and in any case these reflections about meaning can be transplanted into the soil of various other normative standards. I mention the utilitarian philosophy because I wish to modify it by proposing that neither happiness nor meaningfulness alone is adequate for defining the good life. An existence that combines the two is preferable to one in which they conflict. And though there is little reason to believe that achieving happiness or meaning in one's own life necessarily depends upon a dedication to happiness and meaning in life as a whole, living in accordance with this composite ideal can serve as an example of human existence at its best and most significant.

George Bernard Shaw advocates a similar ideal in a passage that is worthy of being memorized. Just a few years after he rejected the interviewer's request for a meaning of the "world-comedy," as quoted earlier, he proclaimed one magnificently in the following words:

> This is the true joy in life, the being used for a purpose recognized by yourself as a mighty one; the being thoroughly worn out before you are thrown on the scrap heap; the being a force of Nature instead of a feverish selfish little clod of ailments and grievances complaining that the world will not devote itself to making you happy. And also the only real tragedy in life is the being used by personally minded men for purposes which you recognize to be base. All the rest is at worst mere misfortune and mortality; this alone is misery, slavery, hell on earth; and the revolt against it is the only force that offers a

man's work to the poor artist, whom our personally minded rich people would so willingly employ as pander, buffoon, beauty monger, sentimentalizer, and the like.[10]

Inspiring as it is, this message nevertheless fails to satisfy in several respects. For one thing, Shaw does not tell us where to find the all-engulfing purpose that instils such joy. Does he think that any humanitarian effort will do? Or does he assume that everyone has the capacity to determine which are truly worthy and which are specious or even base? Many of us in the twentieth century shudder at the succession of massive purposes that have squandered human energies for the ends of bigotry, oppression, and unnecessary suffering. At the same time, Shaw understands the benefits of having a mission in life. Except during wartime, democracies devoted to "life, liberty and the pursuit of happiness" have generally ignored the motivational goods that derive from joint commitment to a mighty cause.

Authoritarian regimes have often made a greater effort to impart a single purpose that would make life meaningful for millions of their citizens. When the totalitarian governments fail, as they usually do, it is because they neglect the equally essential demands for freedom and personal happiness. The ideal integration between meaning and happiness has eluded contemporary society in ways that Shaw could not have foreseen when he wrote at the turn of the century.

Moreover, Shaw does not explain what it is to be "a force of Nature." As human beings, we all incorporate divergent and frequently conflicting elements of what is natural. Making ourselves into a force, rather than a selfish clod, means accentuating one or another of these elements—be it aggressiveness or compassion, self-determination or conformity, hatred or love. These and other tendencies in our nature normally interact as vectors that prevent any one of them from dominating exclusively. Does Shaw believe that the true joy in life, the attaining of what is really important, entails a preferential hierarchy among them? If so, how can it be known and used to order our behavior? If not, should we indiscriminately give free rein to all or any instincts, doing whatever bursts forth, regardless of the consequences?

To answer such questions we would have to formulate a complete and unified theory of human nature. Much of recent anthropology and primatology, piecemeal though this research may as yet be, is devoted to constructing that kind of theory. There is no need for me to summarize the scientific data. Nonetheless, two aspects of our natural being should be mentioned as clues for understanding what it means to preserve and perfect life.

I have introduced this expression in an attempt to find some attitude or way of living that we could accept as that which makes a life significant. The effort will be groundless unless we see ourselves as parts of nature. This in turn implies we *have* a nature—both as examplars of an evolutionary species and as diverse but similar individuals within that species. These two aspects bear further analysis.

Nowadays it has become fashionable among philosophers to deny that there is a human nature. Existentialists who reject the idea that man has any definable essence do well to insist that he is always free to change his condition and thus to modify his being extensively. But these modifications occur within limits established by realities that are given to us and not merely chosen—physical laws, biological determinants of life on this planet, social, historical, and cultural realities to which we are born and through which we must fashion our generic as well as our individual nature.[11]

Coordinates such as these, the facts of our condition as human beings together with our personal modes of responding to them, create a dual nature that each of us possesses. To a large degree, success in life requires having the talent and the courage to be true to one's own nature as it has developed throughout the years. We are not endowed with infinite capacities, and we cannot annihilate the lingering presence of the past. To think otherwise is to live in fantasy. We are able to realize what is in us at any moment only to the extent that we harness forces—often too deep or remote in origin for us to perceive them clearly—that have made us what we are. The first requirement for preserving and perfecting life involves allegiance to the potentialities within us that constitute our nature as individuals. We cannot truly be ourselves if we merely drift with the times, passively submit to other people's desires, or refuse to face up to the implications of what we want and what we do. The *acceptance* of our nature—which does not mean compliant acquiescence in faults that we can remedy—is essential for living a meaningful life, and therefore one that is significant as well. It is because we accept nature that we can improve it. We show respect for what it is even while we alter it in pursuing ideals.

The acceptance of our individual nature is sometimes called "self-love." Traditional religions have often condemned it as a variant of arrogance or hunger for aggrandizement at the expense of others. This assumes that all self-love reduces to selfishness. But that is not the case. On the contrary, self-love can strengthen our capacity to love someone else; and, in general, we cannot love another unless we love ourselves.

Even when it originates as vanity, self-love can become a healthy and commendable attitude. This happens to Mr. Darcy in Jane Austen's novel *Pride and Prejudice*. Though the vain man may seem smug and wholly pleased with his own attributes, he observes himself through the eyes of other people. He tries to gratify his need for self-love through his appearance to them regardless of what he really is or does. If he comes to recognize that self-love cannot be satisfied in a relationship of this sort, he may possibly learn how to make himself *worthy* of approbation. One way of doing this is to act for others in a manner that exceeds his own selfish benefit. To that extent they become separate persons for him rather than mirrors reflecting only himself. He may eventually appreciate the fact that they are autonomous realities and most of what they care about has nothing to do with him. When vanity is transmuted into this greater awareness, self-love remains but now increases, not diminishes, the ability to accept the nature in other people.

Some philosophers have argued that we love others in the same way that we love ourselves. I think they are mistaken. Despite the biblical injunction, we cannot love our neighbor *as* ourselves— for that he is not: we are necessarily different. Through love we accept and bestow value upon whatever it is that makes the neighbor different. And if we managed to love the entire universe, as the nineteenth-century mystic Margaret Fuller said she did, we would love all the myriad properties that distinguish its many components from one another. But are we really able to do this? Much of the world lies beyond our acquaintance and most of it defeats our efforts to appreciate or even understand its inner workings.

For similar reasons we may doubt whether human beings are able to love all of life. And if not, how can they want to preserve and perfect it? Love requires a bestowal of value that unites imagination, intellect, and feeling. But our powers of bestowal are highly circumscribed, and the reach of imagination, intellect, or feeling is always delimited by our cultural and genetic inheritance. Even the saints are bound to some creed that others have manufactured for them, as a kind of uniform that clothes their subtlest intuitions and can always misrepresent the spiritual import of their lives. In wishing to love God by loving all that he has created, we end up loving whatever our conceptual system denotes as "the universe." And in any event, our willingness to love is often impeded by negative feelings beyond our control. Can anyone love, in the sense that he might love himself or another human being, the virus that has invaded his body and will now proceed to kill him?

If we cannot love all living things as the specific reality that each of them is, we can nevertheless treat them as possible *candidates* for love. We thereby experience every life as something that may be seen within its natural context and from its own point of view. Without being able to speak, the murderous virus affirms its need to live with the same urgency that we feel in wanting to destroy it. We have no reason to love this much of animate existence, but in realizing that we attack it merely because we want to stay alive, and not because of any supreme legitimacy on our part, we recognize its equivalent claim, accept it as a kindred being, and thus identify ourselves with it to some degree.

By extension to the cosmos as a whole, this may be what Nietzsche meant by amor fati. It is an ability, as Santayana and possibly Spinoza would say, "to love the love in [everything]."[12] I interpret this conception to imply that all things love themselves inasmuch as they do what they do as a means of preserving and perfecting their own being. We may not, and in fact we cannot, share or even fathom their varied and conflicting interests, many of which are actually self-defeating. But we are capable of imagining that there is in them something equivalent to what we experience, even if it is only self-love. And why should one deny that we can love that aspect of reality?

In making this act of acceptance, we recognize the ontological indefeasibility of other creatures, bestowing value upon it even when we try to annihilate them. We assert an a priori good will toward nature in all its variations. What we affirm is existence seeking to preserve and possibly improve itself in each occurrence. To love the love in everything is to acknowledge this as a trope that may be universal and to treat it as something to which we give importance. That bestowal need not happen; on most occasions it does not happen. But to that extent, I wish to say, we all neglect a potentiality in our being and lose out on opportunities to create a more significant life for ourselves.

I do not speak as one who has succeeded in this endeavor. Love of the love in everything, acceptance of the inherent nature of all things or even those that are alive, is an achievement that few human beings can honestly hope to attain. It is nevertheless an ideal that has mattered to many people—most obviously to the saints and mystics, but also to persons who feel no need for doctrinal affiliations. In pursuing this ideal, we add a dimension to our experience that supplements our practical or material necessities. We thereby enlarge our being as self-regarding animals and align ourselves with that much of nature that seeks to protect and perfect life. Small and isolated as we may be, we thereby establish our oneness with the rest of the universe.

Pantheistic religions have often described this love of love as attunement to a divinity that pervades nature and is present in us even if we repudiate it. Those who feel the force in such religions will understand why I say that accepting one's own nature as well as the nature in everything else contributes to a significant life. But for many others, this idea may seem outrageous. For one thing, they will insist, it implies no particular course of action. It prescribes no deeds that are specifically good in themselves or necessarily beneficial to others. The two types of acceptance to which I have referred would seem to be nothing but attitudes toward life, feelings that may not lead to any detailed effort that changes the world and possibly makes it better. How then can they illuminate what is significant in life? How can we claim to have found a means of exploiting imaginative and creative capabilities that really matter?

This line of criticism is apt and wholly appropriate. All the same, it is short-sighted: it forgets that our strongest attitudes will normally appear in our behavior. Love is emotion that issues into action and often employs the greatest powers of creativity. Directing itself to life in general, it will engender whatever purposiveness is needed under the circumstances. If we love the love in everything, we recognize that all of life is searching for its own meaning and we act accordingly. By enabling others to make their lives more meaningful, we make our own significant. To the degree that we realize this faculty in ourselves, our lives and our experiences truly matter, as much as anything can.

Being a pluralist, I have no desire to specify which conduct is always and uniquely commendable. Nor is there any need to do so. The calamities that human beings have inflicted on themselves are not ordinarily caused by those who have the reverence for life that I am describing. On the other hand, this attitude's importance in the universe should not be overestimated. Nothing in heaven or earth will totally free us from our dependence on the material fate that governs all existence. Once we digest this truth, however, we may learn how to live with our limitations and to cultivate a love that fulfills our nature. To that extent, we not only endure our precarious condition: we complete and partly surmount it.

I previously mentioned Tolstoy's assertion that he learned how to live by observing the simple faith of Russian peasants. Without swallowing the various theses that Tolstoy uses to package his kind of faith, we may agree that even people who have become alienated from their "consciousness of life" can learn how to live. It is not something we learn in the way that we learn how to do mathematics or master a computer program. It would not be a suitable subject for earning credits at a university, and the usual how-to book will not help us very much.

Tolstoy was therefore right when he sought to emulate the attitude of ordinary people working on the land. Philosophy may help to cleanse our thinking, but only in experience itself, in stumbling through life and reflecting about our moments of joy and despair, can we learn how to live. It is something that we all do imperfectly, and the man who concludes that nothing matters has failed in it completely. To help him, we must strengthen his self-love and his love of others. Many things will then be meaningful to him that were not otherwise. If he can identify with the love in everything, including himself, his life will seem significant to him. And indeed it will be.

But what if someone is only interested in "having a good time," pursuing mindless pleasures or the honeyed delights of *la douceur de vivre?* What if he wishes to refine a talent or technique that will never benefit others? What if he merely wants to purify his soul and attain esoteric insights that cannot be communicated to anyone else? These are exotic islands in the ocean of life, and they may sometimes be very beautiful. They can certainly be meaning-ful, and they can even illustrate how some individuals may approach perfection within a limited compartment of their being. But otherwise, their significance will be virtually nil. They do not reveal how to fulfill one's nature. As Socrates says about the good man in a bad society who withdraws and takes "the shelter of a wall," this partial response may be all he can do under the circumstances and yet he is not functioning fully or reaching his ultimate potentiality.

But surely, one might say, a person could very well insist that he does not want to realize his potential or live what I call a significant life. Like all achievements, it demands sacrifices, and he may be unwilling to make them. A man or woman may prefer the commonplace goods of a selfish but happy existence, or even one that is merely contented, given over to bodily comforts and so undistinguished that most of us might consider it meaningless. If we are faithful to our own pluralism, we cannot maintain that such people have necessarily made a wrong decision. Though our ideals are rooted in human nature, they cannot command allegiance. Those who spurn them are always free to choose their own destiny. A good society will tolerate all ways of life, and all deviations from someone else's, as long as the rights of others are respected.

❋

In attempting to determine what might constitute a life that is both meaningful and significant, I have left unanswered many questions about "the meaning of life." I saw no direct way of handling them. Nevertheless, these questions cannot be dismissed entirely. They linger as a permanent striving to move beyond the barriers of our intellect. Even at the risk of talking nonsense, human beings will always speculate about the universe in its totality. I have no desire to impede that endeavor. I only ask that all proposed solutions about the meaning of life remain coherent with our knowledge of what it is to have a meaningful life. For in that area of exploration we can make definite progress, and perhaps the meaning of life is the life of meaning, the attaining and augmenting of meaningful life in ourselves and in life as a whole.

If I am right in this surmise, we fulfill our basic humanity whenever we live a life that has significance in terms of life itself. Those who love the love in everything, who care about this bestowal and devote themselves to it, experience an authentic love of life. It is a love that yields its own kind of happiness and affords many opportunities for joyfulness. Can anything in nature or reality be better than that?

NOTES

INTRODUCTION

1. Bernard Shaw, *Sixteen Self Sketches* (London: Constable, 1949), pp. 90–91.

2. Quoted in Ernest Jones, M.D., *The Life and Work of Sigmund Freud* (New York: Basic Books, 1953–57), 3:465.

3. Leo Tolstoy, *Confession*, trans. David Patterson (New York: W. W. Norton, 1983), p. 26.

4. Ibid., pp. 27–28.

5. Ibid., pp. 28–29.

6. Ibid., p. 51.

7. Ibid.

8. Ibid., p. 52.

9. Ibid., p. 55.

10. On this, see the chapter on Tolstoy in Karl Stern, *The Flight from Woman* (New York: Paragon House, 1985), pp. 173–97. For an analysis of Tolstoy's *Confession*, see Antony Flew, "What Does It Mean to Ask: 'What is the Meaning of Life?'" in his *The Presumption of Atheism and Other Philosophical Essays on God, Freedom and Immortality* (New York: Barnes & Noble, 1976), pp. 155–67.

11. Thomas Hobbes, *Leviathan*, part I, chap. 13.

12. Ludwig Wittgenstein, *Notebooks 1914–1916*, 2d ed., ed. G. H. von Wright and G. E. M. Anscombe, trans. G. E. M. Anscombe (Chicago: The

University of Chicago Press, 1979), pp. 73e–74e; see also his *Tractatus Logico-Philosophicus*, trans. D. F. Pears and B. F. McGuinness (London: Routledge & Kegan Paul, 1961), pp. 149–51. For a commentary that detects an implied reference to Tolstoy in the relevant passage, see G. E. M. Anscombe, *An Introduction to Wittgenstein's Tractatus* (London: Hutchinson University Library, 1963), p. 170.

13. Douglas Adams, *The Hitchhiker's Guide to the Galaxy* (New York: Pocket Books, 1981), p. 181.

CHAPTER 1. THE MEANING OF LIFE

1. Friedrich Nietzsche, *Ecce Homo*, in his *On the Genealogy of Morals and Ecce Homo*, trans. Walter Kaufmann and R. J. Hollingdale (New York: Vintage Books, 1967), p. 258.

2. There are lengthier analyses of the relationship among these three philosophers in my trilogy *The Nature of Love* (Chicago: The University of Chicago Press, 1984–87). See volume 2, *The Nature of Love: Courtly and Romantic*, pp. 393–411, 443–68; and volume 3, *The Nature of Love: The Modern World*, pp. 65–94.

3. See Paul Edwards, "Why?" in *The Meaning of Life*, ed. E. D. Klemke (New York: Oxford University Press, 1981), pp. 227–40.

4. William James, *Pragmatism: A New Name for Some Old Ways of Thinking* (New York: Longmans, Green, 1910), pp. 106–7.

5. *The Dialogues of Plato*, trans. B. Jowett (New York: Random House, 1937), 2:14.

6. On this, see A. J. Ayer, "The Claims of Philosophy," in *Philosophy of the Social Sciences*, ed. Maurice Natanson (New York: Random House, 1963), pp. 475–79; and Robert Nozick, *Philosophical Explanations* (Cambridge: Harvard University Press, 1981), pp. 588ff. For a contrasting view, see Reinhold Niebuhr, "The Self and Its Search for Ultimate Meaning," in *The Meaning of Life*, ed. Klemke, pp. 41–45.

7. On this, see the following essays in *The Meaning of Life: Questions, Answers and Analysis*, ed. Steven Sanders and David R. Cheney (Englewood Cliffs, N.J.: Prentice-Hall, 1980): Kurt Baier, "The Meaning of Life," pp. 47–63; R. W. Hepburn, "Questions about the Meaning of Life," pp. 113–28. See also Ilham Dilman, "Professor Hepburn on Meaning in Life," *Religious Studies* 3 (Apr. 1968): 547–54; and his essay "Life and Meaning," in Ilham Dilman and D. Z. Phillips, *Sense and Delusion* (New York: Humanities Press, 1971), pp. 1–39.

8. Cf. John Wisdom, "The Meanings of the Questions of Life," in his *Paradox and Discovery* (Oxford: Basil Blackwell, 1965), pp. 38–42.

9. Albert Camus, "An Absurd Reasoning," in his *The Myth of Sisyphus and Other Essays*, trans. Justin O'Brien (New York: Vintage Books, 1955), p. 21.

10. Thomas Nagel, "The Absurd," in his *Mortal Questions* (Cambridge: Cambridge University Press, 1979), p. 21.

11. Ibid., p. 23.

12. Thomas Nagel, *The View from Nowhere* (New York: Oxford University Press, 1986), p. 223.

13. Simone de Beauvoir, *The Ethics of Ambiguity,* trans. Bernard Frechtman (New York: Philosophical Library, 1948), p. 129.

14. *Leaves of Grass* (1891–92), 32.

CHAPTER 2. THE MEANING OF DEATH

1. George Santayana, "A Long Way Round to Nirvana; or Much Ado about Dying," in his *Some Turns of Thought in Modern Philosophy: Five Essays* (New York: Charles Scribner's Sons, 1933), pp. 98–101.

2. See Martin Heidegger, *Being and Time,* sections 50–53.

3. For Heidegger on death, see E. F. Kaelin, *Being and Time: A Reading for Readers* (Tallahassee: Florida State University, 1988), pp. 154–65; Michael Gelven, *A Commentary on Heidegger's Being and Time* (New York: Harper and Row, 1970), pp. 137–58. See also Paul Edwards, *Heidegger on Death: A Critical Evaluation* (La Salle, Ill.: The Hegeler Institute, 1979). For Heidegger on "authentic existence," see Gelven, *Commentary,* pp. 159–72.

4. Jean-Paul Sartre, *Being and Nothingness,* trans. Hazel E. Barnes (New York: Washington Square Press, 1966), pp. 682–83. For Sartre's views on death as well as Heidegger's, see Jacques Choron, *Death and Western Thought* (New York: Collier Books, 1963), pp. 230–54.

5. Sartre, *Being and Nothingness,* p. 678. Italics deleted.

6. Ibid., p. 690.

7. Quoted in Simone de Beauvoir, *Adieux: A Farewell to Sartre,* trans. Patrick O'Brian (New York: Pantheon, 1984), p. 432.

8. Nagel, *The View from Nowhere,* p. 228.

9. Richard Wilbur, "The Genie in the Bottle," in *Mid-Century American Poets,* ed. John Ciardi (New York: Twayne, 1950), p. 7.

10. "Do Not Go Gentle into That Good Night," in *The Collected Poems of Dylan Thomas, 1934–1952* (New York: New Directions, 1971), p. 128.

11. On the acceptance of death, see also Richard Wollheim, *The Thread of Life* (Cambridge: Harvard University Press, 1984), pp. 281–83.

12. For a different, though complementary analysis, see Derek Parfit, *Reasons and Persons* (Oxford: Oxford University Press, 1986), pp. 174–77.

13. *As You Like It,* Act IV, scene i.

14. Quoted in Choron, *Death and Western Thought,* p. 258.

15. T. S. Eliot, "A Dedication to My Wife," in his *Collected Poems 1909–1962* (New York: Harcourt, Brace & World, 1963), p. 221.

CHAPTER 3. THE CREATION OF MEANING

1. George Santayana, "A Brief History of My Opinions," in *The Philosophy of Santayana,* ed. Irwin Edman (New York: Modern Library, 1936), p. 8.

2. See Rudolf Carnap, "The Overcoming of Metaphysics through Logical

Analysis of Language," in *Heidegger and Modern Philosophy: Critical Essays*, ed. Michael Murray (New Haven: Yale University Press, 1978), pp. 23–24. For a more sympathetic analysis of Heidegger's views, see, in the same volume, Stanley Rosen, "Thinking about Nothing," pp. 116–37.

3. See Martin Heidegger, "What Is Metaphysics?" in *Basic Writings from Being and Time (1927) to The Task of Thinking (1964)*, ed. David Farrell Krell (New York: Harper and Row, 1977), pp. 71–112.

4. Tom Stoppard, *Rosencrantz and Guildenstern Are Dead* (New York: Grove Press, 1968), p. 128. The two sets of three ellipsis points are in the original text.

5. "Notes on Talks with Wittgenstein," appended to Ludwig Wittgenstein, "A Lecture on Ethics," trans. Max Black, *The Philosophical Review* 74, No. 1 (Jan. 1965): 12. See also Michael Murray, "Wittgenstein on Heidegger on Being and Dread," in *Heidegger and Modern Philosophy*, pp. 80–83.

6. Albert Einstein, in *Living Philosophies* (New York: Simon & Schuster, 1931), p. 6.

7. William James, "Is Life Worth Living?" in his *Essays on Faith and Morals* (New York: New American Library, 1974), p. 19.

8. Baruch de Spinoza, *Ethics*, in *The Collected Works of Spinoza*, ed. and trans. Edwin Curley (Princeton: Princeton University Press, 1985), vol. 1, pt. 3, prop. 7.

9. For recent discussions about the nature of ideals, see John Kekes, *The Examined Life* (Lewisburg, Pa.: Bucknell University Press, 1988), pp. 77–94; and Robert Nozick, *The Examined Life: Philosophical Meditations* (New York: Simon & Schuster, 1989), pp. 279–85.

CHAPTER 4. LIVES OF MEANING AND SIGNIFICANCE

1. John Stuart Mill, *Autobiography*, in *John Stuart Mill: A Selection of His Works*, ed. John M. Robson (New York: Odyssey Press, 1966), p. 279.

2. Ibid., p. 286.

3. John Stuart Mill, *Utilitarianism*, in *John Stuart Mill: A Selection of His Works*, ed. Robson, p. 161.

4. On Mill's ideas about happiness, see Fred R. Berger, *Happiness, Justice and Freedom: The Moral and Political Philosophy of John Stuart Mill* (Berkeley: University of California Press, 1984), pp. 30–120, 281–89. On the nature of happiness, see Elizabeth Telfer, *Happiness* (London: Macmillan, 1980); Paul W. Taylor, *Principles of Ethics: An Introduction* (Belmont, Calif.: Wadsworth, 1975), pp. 129–43; and Kekes, *The Examined Life*, pp. 161–73.

5. For different ideas about an overall "plan of life," see *Aristotle's Eudemian Ethics: Books I, II, and VIII*, trans. Michael Woods (Oxford: Clarendon Press, 1982), book I, chap. 2 and pp. 52–53; Robert Nozick, *Anarchy, State, and Utopia* (New York: Basic Books, 1974), pp. 50–51; John Rawls, *A Theory of Justice* (Cambridge: Harvard University Press, 1971), pp. 407ff; and Josiah Royce, *The Philosophy of Loyalty*, in *The Basic Writings of Josiah Royce*, ed. John J. McDermott (Chicago: The University of Chicago Press, 1969), 2:920–23.

6. Richard Taylor, "The Meaning of Human Existence," in *Values in Conflict: Life, Liberty, and the Rule of Law*, ed. Burton M. Leiser (New York: Macmillan, 1981), p. 24. See also Richard Taylor, "Time and Life's Meaning," in *Reflective Wisdom: Richard Taylor on Issues That Matter*, ed. John Donnelly (Buffalo: Prometheus, 1989), pp. 38–47; and Richard Taylor, *Good and Evil: A New Direction* (Buffalo: Prometheus, 1984), pp. 256–68.

7. Taylor, "The Meaning of Human Existence," p. 9.

8. Ibid., p. 10.

9. William James, "What Makes a Life Significant?" in his *Essays on Faith and Morals*, pp. 308–9.

10. Ibid., p. 304.

11. *Henry IV*, Pt. 2, Act III, scene i.

12. See R. M. Hare, " 'Nothing Matters,' " in *The Meaning of Life: Questions, Answers and Analysis*, ed. Sanders and Cheney, pp. 97–103.

13. For further discussion of self-fulfillment in relation to meaning in life, see Joel Feinberg, "Absurd Self-Fulfillment," in *Philosophy and the Human Condition*, 2d ed., ed. Tom L. Beauchamp, Joel Feinberg, James M. Smith (Englewood Cliffs: Prentice-Hall, 1989), pp. 586–605.

CONCLUSION

1. On this, see David Wiggins, "Truth, Invention and the Meaning of Life," in his *Needs, Values, Truth: Essays in the Philosophy of Value* (Oxford: Basil Blackwell, 1987), pp. 88ff; and Marvin Kohl, "Meaning of Life and Happiness: A Preliminary Outline," *Dialectics and Humanism* 4 (1981): 39–43.

2. Thornton Wilder, *Our Town* (New York: Avon Books, 1975), pp. 138–39.

3. See Paul Tillich, "The Eternal Now," in *The Meaning of Death*, ed. Herman Feifel (New York: McGraw-Hill, 1959), pp. 30–38.

4. *Hippolytus*, 189.

5. Wittgenstein, *Tractatus Logico-Philosophicus*, p. 149; see also Warren Shibles, "Wittgenstein," in his *Death: An Interdisciplinary Analysis* (Whitewater, Wis.: The Language Press, 1974), pp. 69–80. For doubts about the superior goodness of a future life, see A. J. Ayer, *The Meaning of Life and Other Essays* (London: Weidenfeld & Nicolson, 1990), pp. 203–4.

6. Wittgenstein, *Notebooks 1914–1916*, p. 75e; see also his *Tractatus Logico-Philosophicus*, p. 147.

7. Byron, *Euthanasia*; Sophocles, *Oedipus at Colonus*, 1225—both quoted approvingly in Arthur Schopenhauer, *The World as Will and Representation*, trans. E. F. J. Payne (New York: Dover, 1966), 2:587–88.

8. Nagel, "Death," in his *Mortal Questions*, p. 2.

9. For further discussions of Nagel's position, see Mary Mothersill, "Death," in *Life and Meaning: A Reader*, ed. Oswald Hanfling (Oxford: Basil Blackwell, 1987), pp. 83–92; and Bernard Williams, "The Makropulos Case: Reflections on the Tedium of Immortality," in *Problems of the Self: Philosophical*

Papers 1956–1972 (Cambridge: Cambridge University Press, 1973), pp. 87–89ff.

10. Bernard Shaw, "Epistle Dedicatory to Arthur Bingham Walkley," in *Man and Superman: A Comedy and a Philosophy* (New York: Brentano's, 1905), pp. xxxi–xxxii.

11. On the concept of human nature, see Oswald Hanfling, *The Quest for Meaning* (New York: Basil Blackwell, 1988), pp. 109–64; and Kekes, *The Examined Life*, pp. 31–44.

12. George Santayana, "Ultimate Religion," in *The Philosophy of Santayana*, ed. Edman, p. 581.

INDEX

Absurd, concept of the, 17,
    33–41, 57–58, 60
Adams, Douglas, 15, 150
Amor fati, 21–23, 144–45
Anscombe, G. E. M., 150
Anxiety, ontological, 51–53,
    74, 76–80, 85
Aquinas, 32
Aristotle, 32, 83, 107, 152
Austen, Jane, 143
Authenticity, 52–53
Ayer, A. J., 150, 153

Bach, 83, 91
Bacon, Francis, 10–11
Baier, Kurt, 150
Beauvoir, Simone de, 41, 56,
    151
Beethoven, 91, 117
Berger, Fred R., 152
Bergman, Ingmar, 131
Bonaparte, Marie, 2
Buddha, 6
Byron, 137, 153

Campbell, Joseph, 131
Camus, Albert, 34–36,
    38–39, 110, 112,
    122–23, 137, 150
Capp, Al, 52

Carnap, Rudolf, 74–75, 151
Chardin, Jean-Baptiste, 83
Choron, Jacques, 151
Compassion, 20, 103, 118,
    125, 128
Comte, Auguste, 89
Conrad, Joseph, 42
Cosmic plan, 31–33, 37–38
Cyrano de Bergerac, 99

Death, 18, 46–72, 78–79,
    131–32
    fear of, 6, 10, 61–70, 78
Death drive, concept of,
    49–51, 66–67
Dewey, John, 27–28, 89
Dilman, Ilham, 150
Dostoyevsky, 13, 21

Ecclesiastes, 6
Edwards, Paul, 150–51
Einstein, Albert, 83, 152
Eliot, T. S., 70, 151
Epicurus, 62
Euripides, 134, 153

Feinberg, Joel, 153
Flew, Antony, 149
Freud, Sigmund, 2–3, 21, 42,
    49, 51, 66–67, 71, 93

155

Fuller, Margaret, 144

Gandhi, Mohandas, 5
Gelven, Michael, 151

Hanfling, Oswald, 154
Happiness, 4, 12–14, 20, 45,
    99, 101–5, 115–16,
    119, 120, 125, 127, 128,
    132, 140–41, 148
Hare, R. M., 122–23, 153
Haydn, 83
Hegel, 18–19, 21–23, 62,
    97–98, 140
Heidegger, Martin, 35,
    51–53, 55, 57, 59, 61,
    74–77, 151–52
Hepburn, R. W., 150
Hobbes, 10, 89, 149
Homer, 137
Human nature, 3–4, 58–59,
    65, 89–90, 93–94ff.,
    99–100, 118–21, 127,
    141–44
Hume, 33–34, 76, 89

Ideals, 17–19, 22–23, 25, 43,
    53, 90–100, 103, 108,
    114–15, 120–22,
    140–41, 145
    love of, 98–99
Imagination, 7, 45, 91, 95,
    97, 99, 103, 108–9,
    119, 132, 144, 146
Immortality, 18, 25, 68, 119,
    134–35

Instincts, 65, 70–71, 85–87,
    89
Ives, Charles, 83

James, William, 24, 48,
    85–87, 89, 113–14,
    150, 152–53
Johnson, Samuel, 124
Jones, Ernest, 149
Joyce, James, 124

Kaelin, E. F., 151
Kekes, John, 152, 154
King, Martin Luther, 5
Kohl, Marvin, 153
Kübler-Ross, Elisabeth,
    61

Leibniz, 76
Life
    love of, 131–48
    meaning in, xi, 38–47, 72,
        82, 88–89, 99,
        101–29, 131–48
    meaning of, xi, 1–10,
        13–15, 17–47, 72,
        88, 106–7, 148
    plan of, 107
    purpose in, 25, 28–30,
        105–7, 109
    purpose of, 25, 28–30
    reverence for, 89, 129, 146
    as a tragedy, 11–14, 18–23
    value of, 43, 73–74,
        86–88, 96–97,
        135–39

Living in eternity, 14,
134–35
Living in time, 55–60, 122,
124, 133–35
Love, 24, 43, 65–66, 70, 82,
85, 98–99, 106,
141–46. *See also* Life,
love of
Lucretius, 62–63

Marcel, Gabriel, 70
Meaning. *See also* Life,
meaning in; Life,
meaning of
creation of, 41–47,
72–100
modes of, 90, 99, 142–46
two senses of, 23–24,
105
Mill, John Stuart, 89, 102–4,
115, 117, 152
Mishima, Yukio, 71
Mortimer, John, 135
Mothersill, Mary, 153
Munch, Edvard, 22
Murray, Michael, 152

Nagel, Thomas, 34–35, 39,
58–59, 137, 150–51,
153
Nazi ideology, 128–29
Niebuhr, Reinhold, 150
Nietzsche, 2, 18, 21–23, 88,
145, 150
Nihilism, 33, 40
"Nothing matters," 33ff., 39,
43, 80, 122–28
Nothingness, 51, 55, 61–63,
74–81
Nozick, Robert, 150, 152

Olivier, Laurence, 99

Parfit, Derek, 151
Perfection, concept of,
93–97, 99, 117,
120–22, 132, 139,
143
Phillips, D. Z., 150
Plato, 15, 20, 25–28, 32, 46,
62, 83, 94–98, 109–10,
134, 150
Purpose, 13–14, 17, 25–33,
45, 59, 90–91, 97, 99,
146. *See also* Life,
purpose in; Life,
purpose of

Quine, W. V., 3

Rawls, John, 152
Religious approaches, 8–9,
11–13, 18–19, 24, 29,
31–32, 37–38, 40, 43,
51, 62, 72–73, 81, 83,
96, 106, 135–36, 144,
146–47
Richards, I. A., 15
Rosen, Stanley, 152
Rousseau, 81
Royce, Josiah, 152

Santayana, George, 49–50,
    73, 80, 89, 97, 145,
    151, 154
Sartre, Jean-Paul, 34, 53–61,
    74, 77, 112, 151
Schopenhauer, 6, 18–23,
    63–65, 117, 128, 153
Schweitzer, Albert, 129
Shakespeare, 11, 59, 70–71,
    84, 99, 116, 138, 153
Shaw, George Bernard, 1–2,
    67, 140–42, 149, 154
Shibles, Warren, 153
Significance, *xi*, 43, 101,
    113–29, 132, 139–48
Socrates, 6, 15, 46, 83, 104,
    147
Sophocles, 137, 153
Spinoza, 88, 128, 145, 152
Stein, Gertrude, 14
Stendhal, 82
Stern, Karl, 149
Stoppard, Tom, 75, 152

Taylor, Harriet, 103
Taylor, Paul W., 152
Taylor, Richard, 107–11, 153
Telfer, Elizabeth, 152

Thomas, Dylan, 61, 151
Tillich, Paul, 134, 153
Toklas, Alice B., 14
Tolstoy, 5–10, 43, 92, 147,
    149

Value, 2–3, 17–18, 22,
    24–28, 36–37, 40, 42,
    44, 54, 63, 69–70,
    73–74, 80, 87–91,
    97–98, 104–6, 117,
    121, 123, 127–28, 136,
    137–38, 144, 145. *See
    also* Life, value of

Whitehead, Alfred North,
    134
Whitman, Walt, 45
Wiggins, David, 153
Wilbur, Richard, 59, 151
Wilder, Thornton, 133, 153
Williams, Bernard, 153
Wisdom, John, 150
Wittgenstein, Ludwig,
    13–14, 80, 81n.,
    149–50, 152–53
Wollheim, Richard, 151
Wonder, 80–85, 89